MW00978626

FAMILY ADVENTURE GUIDE™

MISSOURI

"The Family Adventure Guide series . . . enables parents to turn family travel into an exploration."

—Alexandra Kennedy, Editor, *FamilyFun* magazine

MISSOURI

FAMILY ADVENTURE GUIDE™

by

JANE COSBY

A VOYAGER BOOK

The
Globe
Pequot
Press

OLD SAYBROOK, CONNECTICUT

Family Adventure Guide is a trademark of The Globe Pequot Press, Inc.
Cover illustration by Lainé Roundy

Library of Congress Cataloging-in-Publication Data

Cosby, Jane.
    Missouri : family adventure guide / by Jane Cosby. — 1st ed.
       p.   cm. — (Family adventure guide series)
    Includes index.
    "A voyager book."
    ISBN 1-56440-964-3
    1. Missouri—Guidebooks. 2. Family recreation—Missouri—
Guidebooks. I. Title. II. Series.
    F464.3.C67   1997
    917.7804—dc20   96–30531
                                                     CIP

Manufactured in the United States of America
First Edition/First Printing

To Randy, who taught me how to write,
and Mike and Annie,
who make traveling so much fun.

MISSOURI

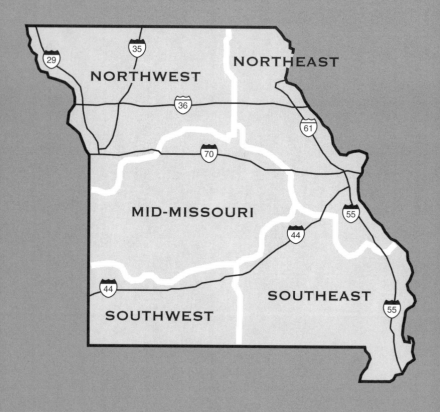

CONTENTS

TOP TEN FREE FAMILY ADVENTURES IN MISSOURI

1. St. Louis Zoo, St. Louis
2. St. Louis Science Center, St. Louis
3. Grant's Farm, Affton
4. Conservation Nature Centers in St. Louis, Blue Springs, Springfield, and Jefferson City
5. Johnson Shut-Ins State Park, south of Graniteville
6. Mark Twain National Forest, southern region of state
7. National Scenic Riverways, southeastern region of state
8. Bass Pro Shops Outdoor World, Springfield
9. Katy Trail State Park, St. Charles to Sedalia
10. Kaleidoscope and Hallmark Visitor Center, Kansas City

INTRODUCTION

I've lived in Missouri all my life and have come to appreciate the incredible opportunities for recreation throughout the state, from St. Joseph to Joplin to St. Louis and all points in between. From metropolitan glamour and glitz to the friendliness and instant familiarity so often found in small towns, Missouri truly has something for everyone.

This book is the result of my family's travels across the state, and many interviews with Missouri parents. The book is divided into five regions, each of which is introduced by a map that highlights the towns you'll want to visit and lists attractions and events you won't want to miss. In the text, the towns are arranged in a way that should make it easier to reach attractions while driving through a region.

As you may know, Missouri is called the Show Me State. One supposed origin of the motto is a turn-of-the-century state representative who said, "Frothy eloquence neither convinces nor satisfies me. I am from Missouri. You have got to show me."

I sincerely hope this guidebook is eloquent enough to convince you to explore Missouri and informative enough to ensure that your travels are hassle-free, and that it succeeds in showing you the many good times waiting for your family in this beautiful state.

Northeast Region

The central and northern parts of this region are primarily rural and include an excellent large lake for outdoor recreation, the town of Hannibal sitting on the Mississippi River welcoming tourists to formative places in the life of author Mark Twain, and quaint little sleepy towns along the Mississippi where time seems to stand still. As you travel south in the region you'll find St. Louis and the surrounding suburbs, which together form the largest metropolitan area in the state. From the vibrant downtown area to the many historic neighborhoods and the outlying suburban communities, there are dozens of family attractions, recreational opportunities, and entertainment options, many of them free or low cost. South and west of St. Louis you'll find small towns, nature preserves, and large parks offering outdoor recreation of all types.

MEXICO

In this small rural town, you'll find several interesting attractions and a playground and picnic area in **Robert S. Green Park**, 501 South Muldrow. The **Audrain Historical Society at Graceland** offers historical artifacts housed in a stately mansion once visited by Ulysses S. Grant. Antique dolls, dishes, tools, and clothing are displayed throughout the house. The **Audrain Country School** offers a glimpse of rural school life in the early part of the twentieth century with desks, books, slates, and games from schools throughout the county, as well as an out-

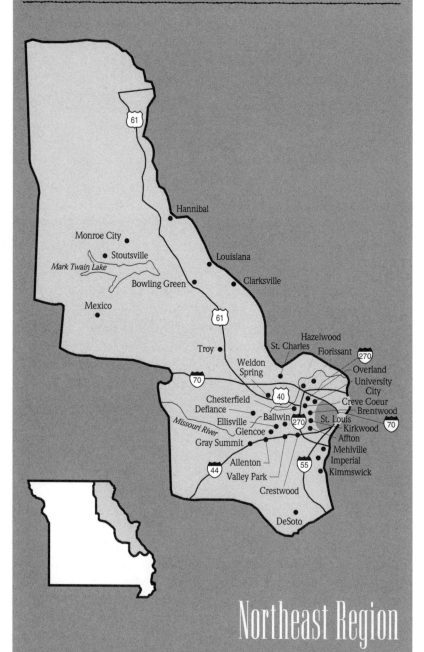

61

Hannibal

Monroe City •
• Stoutsville

Mark Twain Lake

Louisiana

Bowling Green

Clarksville

Mexico •

61

Troy •

Hazelwood
St. Charles
Florissant

270

Weldon
Spring

Overland

40

University
City

Chesterfield

Creve Coeur

Defiance

Brentwood

Missouri River

Ballwin

270

Ellisville

St. Louis

70

Glencoe

Kirkwood

Gray Summit

Affton

Allenton

Mehlville

44

Valley Park

55

Imperial

Kimmswick

Crestwood

DeSoto

Northeast Region

house out back. At the **American Saddle Horse Museum** you'll find equestrian memorabilia and paintings. Admission for all three is $2.00 for adults, 50 cents for children. Open Tuesday through Saturday 1:00 to 4:00 P.M. and Sunday 2:00 to 5:00 P.M., April through December. Call (573) 581–3910.

Also noteworthy is **Scattering Fork Outdoor Center,** Route 3 just southeast of town, a nonprofit educational center that uses the outdoors as a classroom for group activities and nature programs. For information about their programs call (573) 581–3003. The **Miss Missouri Pageant** is held at the **Missouri Military Academy,** 204 Grand Avenue, every June. You can come and watch while contestants from all over the state compete for the coveted title. Tours of the school can be arranged if you call in advance. Call (573) 581–2765.

STOUTSVILLE

To the north is **Mark Twain State Park** on Highway 107, overlooking the 18,600-acre **Mark Twain Lake.** Fishing and boating are popular pastimes in these parts. The park covers almost 3,000 acres and offers hiking trails, fifty-six developed campsites, swimming beaches, picnic areas, and two full-service marinas. A waterfowl refuge along Middle Fork Salt River is an ideal location for bird-watching and wildlife viewing. The M. W. Boudreaux Visitor Center offers a good vantage point for bird-watching. Open daily 10:00 A.M. to 5:00 P.M. late April through November. Call (573) 735–4097.

Inside the park is a museum with the two-room log cabin where Mark Twain, whose given name was Samuel Clemens, was born. Exhibits feature personal belongings and books of the famous author-humorist and present information about his life. Admission is $2.00 for adults, $1.25 for children ages six to twelve. Open daily 10:00 A.M. to 4:00 P.M. Call (573) 565–3449.

At **South Fork Resort,** across from the state park, cabins and motel units are available with boat rentals and boat ramps nearby. Call (573) 565–3500. During Fourth of July weekend you can enjoy the **Mark Twain Lake Rodeo** at the South Spillway Area. Charging bulls, bucking broncos, clowns, bands, food, and fireworks are all part of the show. Call (573) 565–2228.

MONROE CITY

To the east of Stoutsville is **The Landing,** Route J, a resort with camp-grounds, cabins, condos, and a water park. The water park has a giant wave pool, slippery slides, a river, and an adult swim-up bar. The resort also has miniature golf, go-carts, and a playground. Admission to the water park is $9.95 for adults, $7.95 for kids ages twelve and younger. Open daily 11:00 A.M. to 7:00 P.M., but hours vary so call ahead. Open Memorial Day through Labor Day. Call (573) 735–4242.

HANNIBAL

As you travel east toward the Mississippi River you'll reach the little town that Mark Twain propelled to national prominence. Twain grew up in this small hamlet on the banks of the river and featured it in some of his best-loved works of fiction. Today Hannibal offers activities and places of inter-est that take full advantage of its association with America's favorite humorist. Before you visit, spend some time reviewing *The Adventures of Tom Sawyer* and *The Adventures of Huckleberry Finn* with your children. Kids who have read the Mark Twain stories, or seen the movies based on his books, will enjoy viewing the places where the "real" people lived. For information call (573) 221–2477.

There are several ways to get around town. You can hop on the **Hannibal Trolley,** at the corner of Main and Bird Streets, for a tour of all the local attractions. Tickets are $6.00 for adults, $5.50 for seniors, $3.50 for children ages five to twelve. Runs daily 9:00 A.M. to 5:00 P.M. April 15 through October. Call (573) 221–1161.

The **Twainland Express,** 400 North Third Street, offers two tours blending historical facts with humorous stories. Tickets are $6.50 for adults, $4.74 for children ages five to twelve. Runs daily April through October. Call (573) 221–5593. Or try the **Mark Twain Clopper,** for a ride on a horse-drawn wagon. Tickets are $3.00 for adults, $1.50 for chil-dren ages twelve and younger. Call (573) 439–5054.

When you tour the **Mark Twain Boyhood Home,** 208 Hill Street, you'll see where the author grew up and find out about his childhood and the real people behind his characters. Next door is the **Mark Twain Museum and Annex,** where you can view memorabilia, displays and a slide presentation on Twain's life. Across the street is **J.M. Clemens Law Office,** where Clemens's father presided as justice of the peace, and **Pilaster House/Grant's Drug Store,** where the Clemens family lived on the upper level for a short time. Admission for all five buildings is $4.00 for adults, $2.00 for children ages six to twelve. Open daily 9:00 A.M. to 4:00 P.M., extended hours from spring to fall. Call (573) 221–9010.

In the **Becky Thatcher Book and Gift Shop,** 211 Hill Street, you can see two rooms from Laura Hawkins's childhood home. She was Twain's childhood sweetheart and the model for Becky Thatcher. A well-stocked bookshop offers a large selection of Twain's books, in addition to children's classics and souvenirs for the whole family. Free admission. Open daily 9:00 A.M. to 4:00 P.M., extended hours from spring to fall. Call (573) 221–0822.

The **Haunted House on Hill Street,** 215 Hill Street, offers guided tours of twenty-seven wax figures, many of them from Twain's books. One level is devoted to the typical eerie, blood-and-guts fare so often associated with wax museums. Admission $2.00 for adults, $1.00 for children ages six to eleven. Open daily 8:00 A.M. to 5:00 P.M. March through November, open until 8:00 P.M. during summer months. Call (573) 221–2220.

The **Optical Science Center and Museum,** 214 North Main Street, has hands-on exhibits about vision, optic lenses, and the optometry industry. You'll see optical illusions, lenses being made, and more than 500 pairs of glasses. You can also watch a puppet show and a computerized light show. Educational videos about vision are shown in a small theater. Admission is $3.50 for adults, $2.00 for children ages three to ten. Open Monday through Saturday 10:00 A.M. to 6:00 P.M., Sunday 12:00 to 6:00 P.M. April through mid-December. Call (573) 221–2020.

Family diners can check out **Ole Planters Restaurant,** 316 South Main Street, owned by the same family for two generations and offering well-loved family recipes on the menu. Specialties include barbecue ribs, prime rib, and homemade pies. Call (573) 221–4410.

Take a ride on the **Mark Twain Riverboat,** which leaves from the landing at the foot of Center Street. You'll hear an hour-long narration of Twain's adventures and the history and legends of the river. You'll see sights along the river, and you can purchase refreshments at the snack bar.

Tickets are $8.00 for adults, $5.00 for children ages three to twelve. Cruises leave daily at 1:30 P.M. May through October. Additional cruises at 11:00 A.M. and 4:00 P.M. from Memorial Day through Labor Day. Call (573) 221–3222.

Another famous resident is featured at the **Molly Brown Dinner Theater,** 200 North Main Street. "The Unsinkable Molly," who refused to go down with the Titanic, leads a cast in singing and dancing while you enjoy your meal. Tickets for the lunch show are $17.95 for adults, $11.95 for children ages three to twelve. Dinner show tickets are $21.95 for adults, $15.95 for children. For a schedule of shows call (573) 221–8940.

During the summer months, local actors present a two-hour pageant about Mark Twain and his famous characters at the **Mark Twain Outdoor Theater,** Highway 61 South at Clemens Landing. You'll see episodes from *Tom Sawyer, Huckleberry Finn,* and *Life on the Mississippi.* Tickets are $10.00 for adults, $4.00 for children ages three to twelve. Performances are held every evening from June through August and on weekends in the spring and fall. For a schedule call (573) 221–2945.

Also at the landing you'll find **Injun Joe Campgrounds** with a wooded tent area, full hookups, laundry room, pool, water slide, canoe rental, miniature golf, go-carts, batting cages, fishing lake, and a picnic pavilion. Call (573) 985–3581.

Relive the adventure of Tom Sawyer when you explore **Mark Twain Cave,** Highway 79 South. You'll get an hour-long tour as you walk through chilly passageways, read messages marked on cave walls by long-ago visitors, and learn about the outlaws that sometimes hid in this famous cave. Admission is $9.00 for adults, $5.00 for children ages five to twelve; ages four and younger are free. Open daily 9:00 A.M. to 4:00 P.M. Extended hours April to October.

You'll also find **Cameron Cave** at the same location. This cave, which is open for tours during the summer months, is in a natural state and has no artificial lighting. You will explore it by the light of lanterns carried by several of the people in your group. Admission is $11.00 for adults, $6.00 for children ages five to twelve. Open daily, four tours a day from Memorial Day to Labor Day. Reduced admission for tickets to both caves. A campground next to the caves has RV and tent sites, laundry facilities, grocery, and camping supplies. For information about the caves or camping call (800) 527–0304.

Sawyer's Creek Fun Park, Highway 79 South, is a miniature amusement park with bumper boats, a miniature golf course, a kid-size train, and a shooting gallery and arcade. There is a cafe that offers a wonderful view of the river, and several shops (including a Christmas shop) are open year-round. Open daily 10:00 a.m. to dark. Closed in January and February. Call (573) 221–8221.

Every July the town hosts **Tom Sawyer Days** and features the National Fence Painting Championships, a frog-jumping contest, the Tomboy Sawyer Competition, an arts and crafts show, Mississippi Mud Volleyball, live entertainment, and a huge fireworks display on the evening of July Fourth.

Head south the scenic way by driving along Highway 79, parallel to the Mississippi River. It winds through small, quaint river towns and reveals magnificent scenery along the river bluffs.

LOUISIANA

The downtown business district of this small town is on the National Register of Historic Places and features beautiful Victorian architecture. You can get an unobstructed view of the river at **Riverfront Park,** which features cleared fishing areas and a boat ramp for those wishing to put into the river. **Henderson-Riverview Park,** at the crest of Main and Noyes Streets, has picnic facilities and a playground in full view of the Mississippi River at its most magnificent. On the west edge of town you can visit the **Stark Brothers Garden Center,** one of the oldest commercial nurseries in the world. Call (573) 754–3113. For information about the town call (573) 754–5921.

At the **Ted Shanks Conservation Area,** tucked between the Mississippi and Salt Rivers, you'll find a visitor center containing exhibits, displays, and an observation room highlighting the deer, waterfowl, turkeys, and other wildlife that live here. Hiking trails over the levees cross the marsh and wetlands at the junction of the rivers. Fishing, camping, hiking, and canoeing are available. To reach the area take Highway 79, then go east on County Road TT one mile to area entrance. Call (573) 754–6171.

CLARKSVILLE

To the south is this small historic river town whose vantage point on 500-foot bluffs of the Mississippi River attracts tourists and wildlife. At the **Clarksville Visitor Center,** north of town on Highway 79, you can see the workings of Lock and Dam 24, one of the many locks that make the river navigable for barge traffic. There are exhibits on the U.S. Army Corps of Engineers, and you can see how barges are secured during their passage through the lock. There is also a viewing platform with binoculars for watching the birds that come to feed in the area.

Every January and February this town draws bird-watchers from all over who come to see the wintering bald eagles that live and fish along the river bluffs and around the locks. **Eagle Days** are held at the visitor center in late January and feature special activities, guided eagle-viewing tours, and live eagle exhibits. Free admission. Center open daily 10:00 A.M. to 5:00 P.M. May through February. Open Friday, Saturday, and Sunday during March and April. Call (573) 242–3132.

TROY

Cuivre River State Park on Highway 47, encompasses rugged, wooded terrain and Big Sugar Creek. There are more than 6,000 acres in the park, which includes a fifty-five-acre lake, more than 30 miles of trails, and a special campground just for equestrians. There are 110 regular campsites, thirty-two with full hookups available. A visitor center offers displays and trail maps. Center open daily 8:00 A.M. to 4:00 P.M. Call (314) 528–7247.

WELDON SPRING

The **August A. Busch Memorial Conservation Area,** Highway 94, is a 14,000-acre wildlife preserve that offers a mixture of timber, open fields, streams, springs, and lakes. An 8-mile self-guided automobile tour passes through several habitats that provide great opportunities for wildlife viewing. There are gun and bow ranges for target shooters and plenty of areas for fishing. Picnicking and limited hunting are allowed. A lodge (open 6:00 A.M. to 10:00 P.M. from April 1 to September 30) rents boats and has exhibits and a naturalist on staff for anyone interested in the area's ecology. Adjacent to this area is **Weldon Spring Conservation Area,** off Highway B, and together these two preserves have more than 20 miles of hiking trails. Both areas open daily 6:00 A.M. to 6:00 P.M. Call (314) 441–4554.

DEFIANCE

In this small town on the Missouri River you can visit the **Daniel Boone Home,** Highway F, where a real-life American legend lived and died. Costumed guides give a forty-five-minute tour through the restored brick house Daniel spent seven years building after he moved here from Kentucky, completing it in 1810. **Boonesfield Village,** a collection of restored historic buildings surrounding the home, features demonstrations of crafts and household chores from the nineteenth century and a full schedule of interpretive activities. Admission is $5.00 for adults, $3.50 for children ages four to eleven. Open daily 9:00 A.M. to 6:00 P.M. March through October and 9:00 A.M. to 5:00 P.M. November through February. Call (314) 987–2221.

ST. CHARLES

As you head east you'll start to notice the unmistakable signs of suburban sprawl, but there's more here than twentieth-century bedroom communities. In St. Charles, you'll feel as if you have been transported into the past when you stroll along Main Street. Here you'll find ten blocks of charming, restored eighteenth- and nineteenth-century homes, stores, and taverns. This city was the first settlement on the Missouri River and many of the old buildings are restored and open to the public. Lewis and Clark left for their historic journey from here. For information about attractions in the area, stop at the **St. Charles Convention and Visitors Center,** 230 South Main Street, or call (800) 366–2427 or (314) 946–7776.

To really get a feel for life during the period this area was settled, take a tour of the **First Missouri State Capitol State Historic Site,** 200 South Main Street. This building was used by legislators immediately after Missouri came into the Union, while the permanent capital was being constructed in the middle of the new state. The rooms have been restored to their condition during the 1820s, including the residences and store on the ground floor. Park rangers provide an excellent forty-five-minute tour that explores the lives of early legislators and inhabitants of the area. Tour tickets are $2.00 for adults, $1.25 for children ages seven to twelve; ages six and younger are free. There is a free slide show and small exhibit area. Open Monday through Saturday 10:00 A.M. to 5:00 P.M., Sunday 12:00 to 5:00 P.M. Call (314) 946–9282.

You can learn about one of the greatest adventures in American history at the **Lewis and Clark Center,** 701 Riverside Drive. This small museum tells the story of these great explorers through dioramas and artifacts. It's a wonderful museum for school-age children or grown-ups who have an interest in the exploration and settling of the West. Small admission fee. Open daily 10:30 A.M. to 4:30 P.M. Call (314) 947–3199.

The **Goldenrod Showboat,** docked at the south end of Frontier Park on the riverfront, is the last of the musical showboats that once plied our waterways stopping at river towns along the way to entertain folks with singing and dancing. You can eat a buffet meal and then enjoy a musical production in the 350-seat theater on this historic boat. The season runs from April through September and includes several daytime productions specifically for children. Tickets for children's shows range from $4.50 to $8.50. Tickets for evening performances range from $21 to $30 and include dinner. Call (314) 946–2020.

Here you'll also find the eastern end of the longest hiking and biking trail in the state—**The Katy Trail.** The tracks of the Missouri-Kansas-Texas Railroad have been replaced with hardpacked gravel, and the path now provides visitors with access to sleepy little rural communities, scenic views of the Missouri River bluffs, and opportunities to observe the wildlife living along the river corridor. The trail will one day stretch more than 200 miles to Sedalia, and trail sections are being opened up as they are ready. It has a relatively easy grade and is perfect for family bicyclists or hikers. No motorized vehicles are allowed except for wheelchairs. Trail parking is available at Booneslick Road and Main Street. Trail conditions vary with the season and the level of the river, so call before setting out on an extended trip. For trail information call (800) 334–6946 or (314) 949–0809. Bikes can be rented at **The Touring Cyclist,** 104 South Main Street. Call (314) 949–9630.

St. Charles hosts numerous events throughout the year that will interest families. The **Festival of the Little Hills,** held the third weekend in

JANE'S TOP FAMILY ADVENTURES IN THE NORTHEAST REGION

1. Mark Twain Lake, Stoutsville, (573) 735–4097
2. The Katy Trail, St. Charles, (800) 334–6946 or (314) 949–0809
3. Gateway Arch and Jefferson National Expansion Memorial, St. Louis, (314) 425–6010
4. Missouri Botanical Gardens, St. Louis, (314) 577–5100
5. St. Louis Science Center, St. Louis, (314) 289–4444
6. St. Louis Zoo, St. Louis, (314) 781–0900
7. The Magic House, Kirkwood, (314) 822–8900
8. Grant's Farm, Affton, (314) 843–1700
9. Six Flags Over Mid-America, Allenton, (314) 938–4800
10. Purina Farms, Gray Summit, (314) 982–3232

August, is an enormous craft fair with hundreds of booths featuring wares of every description and cost. The **Lewis and Clark Rendezvous,** held the third weekend in May, is a living-history event that offers great opportunities to see how people lived in the early days of this frontier settlement. Reenactors camp out for the weekend on the riverfront and play the parts of fur traders, mountain men, U.S. soldiers, and Indians. Booths sell handmade goods and crafts, and demonstrations include black powder shoots, parades, fife and drum playing, and battle reenactments.

During the holiday season the entire historic downtown area is lighted and offers special seasonal activities for the entire family. **Los Posadas,** the traditional reenactment of Joseph and Mary seeking shelter at the inn, is held the first weekend of December and features music, carolers, a tree lighting ceremony, and a reception afterwards. For information about any of these events call (800) 366–2427 or (314) 946–7776.

For an adventure your kids will love, drive out to the **Golden Eagle Ferry** and take it, car and all, across the river. On the trip across you'll get a great view of the river and the birds that come to feed here, including bald eagles in the wintertime. Be forewarned that on nice spring and fall days the ferry is inundated with tourists and you may wait hours to board. To reach the ferry take Highway 94 north to Highway B, turn west, and follow the signs to the river and the ferry. Toll for the ferry is $4.00 per car. The **Grafton Ferry** can be reached by taking Highway 94 north to Grafton Ferry Road.

The **Marais Temps Clair Conservation Area** has 918 acres in the middle of the Mississippi River flyway and is a great place for bird-watching. You can see large numbers of waterfowl, raptors, and other birds here. To reach the area go north on Highway 94, then east on County Road H. Then go north on Island Road for 2 miles to the area entrance. The area is closed during waterfowl hunting season. Call (314) 441–4554.

HAZELWOOD

When you head east and cross the Missouri River you'll find several inter-esting places in the northern suburbs of St. Louis. Monster trucks were born here and you can visit the most famous one of all at **Big Foot 4×4 Inc.,** 6311 North Lindbergh Boulevard. You can see several versions of the orig-inal Bigfoot, and one is always on display so fans can have their pictures taken next to or underneath it. You can also see the factory where the trucks are built and shop for Bigfoot souvenirs in the gift shop, which fea-tures an extensive collection of monster truck wearables, toys, models, photos, and videos. Free admission. Open Monday through Friday 9:00 A.M. to 5:00 P.M., Saturday 9:00 A.M. to 4:00 P.M. Call (314) 731–2822.

Archers can practice their skill at **Arrow Point Archery,** 111 Taylor Road, where there is a 20-yard range with fifteen lanes. Shooting is $3.00 an hour for adults, $2.50 for children ages fifteen or younger. Call (314) 731–DEER.

FLORISSANT

The **Family Theater Series** is offered at the Florissant Civic Center, Waterford Avenue and Parker Road. Each season national touring companies are brought in to offer children's productions that the entire family can enjoy together. A regular schedule of concerts, musicals, and mysteries are also presented here. For a schedule of shows and ticket prices call (314) 921–5678.

You'll find a great indoor playground at the **Discovery Zone,** 2B Grandview Plaza. Admission is $3.99 for children ages one to three, $5.99 for ages three and older. Call (314) 830–4747.

The Prologue Room at **McDonnell Douglas World Headquarters,** Airport Road and McDonnell Boulevard, provides a mind-boggling view of the history of the company's role in aviation and space exploration. You can see full-size mock-ups of the Mercury and Gemini spacecraft and a full-size harpoon missile. There are models of the F-15 Eagle, F/A 18 Hornet and the DC-3 airliner. It's a must-see for anyone interested in models, the space program, or military and commercial aviation. Free admission. Open during the summer only. Hours vary, so call for information. Call (314) 232–5421.

If flight is your fancy, spend some time browsing in the McDonnell Douglas Gift Shop, 5900 North Lindbergh Boulevard. You'll find clothing, souvenirs, and decorative items emblazoned with the company's products, the most technologically advanced aircraft in the world. Open Tuesday through Friday 10:00 A.M. to 6:00 P.M., Saturday 10:00 A.M. to 3:00 P.M. Call (314) 895–7070.

Sioux Passage County Park, Old Jamestown Road, has 5 miles of wooded trails, campgrounds, and horse trails and offers great opportunities for walks along the Missouri River. You'll also find athletic fields, fishing access to the river, picnic tables and shelters, a children's playground, and tennis courts. Call (314) 889–2863.

ST. LOUIS

Travel farther east and you'll hit the Mississippi River and the city of St. Louis. The city sits just below the confluence of the Mississippi and Missouri Rivers and is famous for its beer, baseball, historic neighborhoods, and original cuisine. This is where ice cream cones, iced tea, hot dogs, and toasted ravioli originated. So don't leave town without sampling the local fare. Since Illinois is just across the river, you might want to check out some of the attractions on that side of the river too. For information about attractions in the area call (800) 325–7962 or (314) 421–1023.

Start your exploration of this city in the downtown area with a visit to the country's tallest monument, **The Gateway Arch,** located on the river-front. Once you get downtown you won't need directions—the Arch dominates the skyline and makes downtown easy to navigate without a map. The Arch grounds and the Old Courthouse across the street form the **Jefferson National Expansion Memorial,** a federal park dedicated to the president who purchased the Louisiana Territory and helped foster the westward expansion of our country.

Underneath the Arch you'll find an outstanding museum explaining the role of the people who conquered the west. The **Museum of Westward Expansion** has an unusual semicircular layout, so talk to a park ranger for a quick orientation before you begin browsing or it may be very confusing to you and your children. The museum has fascinating exhibits illustrated with historic photographs of people and places and artifacts from the period. The rangers offer wonderful interpretive activities to spice up your experience and can answer all your questions.

Be sure to purchase tickets to ride to the observation deck at the top of the Arch when you first come in; you can visit the museum while waiting for your turn to go up. You'll ride in a very small conveyor car to reach the top where you can see all of the downtown area and, on a clear day, 30 miles beyond.

There is a fascinating film on the construction of the Arch that you won't want to miss and an IMAX theater that always offers two different films. Tickets to view all three films and ride to the top are $11.00 for adults, $9.00 for children ages thirteen to sixteen, $4.00 for children ages three to twelve. Individual tickets also can be purchased. Open daily 8:00 A.M. to 10:00 P.M. from Memorial Day to Labor Day, open daily 9:00 A.M. to 6:00 P.M. from September through May.

The **Old Courthouse,** 11 North Fourth Street, is steeped in history and has four galleries detailing the history of the city. You can see exhibits about the fur traders who founded the city, the transportation revolution during the Victorian Age and the city's heyday at the turn of the century. The Dred Scott case originated in this courthouse, and you can learn about this monumental decision on slavery and the part it played in leading our country into the Civil War in the galleries on the west side. Free admission. Open daily 8:00 A.M. to 4:00 P.M. For information about the Arch or the Old Courthouse call (314) 425–6010.

Just north of the Arch is **Laclede's Landing,** an area of nineteenth-century buildings and cobblestone streets with stores, restaurants, and several fascinating small museums. The **National Video Game and Coin-Op Museum,** 801 North Second Street, is a great place for video nuts. This arcade features names and games you may remember and your kids probably never will see anywhere else, like Pac-Man and Donkey Kong and even the first of all video games, Pong. There usually are seventy-five different games on display and for a quarter you and your kids can try your hand at any of these obsolete, but still-fun diversions. Tokens are 25 cents each or twenty-five for $5.00. Open Sunday through Friday 12:00 to 6:00 P.M., Saturday until 10:00 P.M. Call (314) 621–2900.

At the **Dental Health Theater,** 727 North First Street, young kids can view an educational talk, film, and puppet show on proper dental hygiene while sitting on a pink-carpet tongue surrounded by 3-foot-tall teeth. Free admission, but reservations are required. Shows conducted Monday through Friday 9:00 A.M. to 4:00 P.M. Call (314) 241–7391. The **Laclede's Landing Wax Museum,** 720 North Second Street, features more than 150 authentically costumed beeswax figures ranging from Richard Burton and Elizabeth Taylor as Anthony and Cleopatra, to a young, slim Elvis. Be forewarned not to go into the basement, or take your young children down there, unless you want to see the blood, guts, and gore that made wax museums so popular years ago. Hours and admission prices vary with the season, so call (314) 241–1155.

Just west of the landing is the convention center and the **TWA Dome,** 901 North Broadway Avenue, where the **St. Louis Rams** professional football team plays. Tickets are hard to come by—only a few thousand per game are available, at $25 each. These tickets go on sale in the summer for the following season. Call (314) 425–8830.

Getting around downtown is easy and fun on **Metrolink,** the light transit railway that runs between downtown and Lambert St. Louis International Airport. Tickets are $1.00 for adults, 50 cents for children ages five to twelve; ages four and younger are free. Everyone can ride free in the downtown area Monday through Friday from 11:00 A.M. to 2:00 P.M. For a schedule and ticket information call (314) 231–2345.

Down at the river you can take a one-hour narrated sightseeing cruise of Ol' Man River with **Gateway Riverboat Cruises.** Catch the boat from the dock just beneath the Arch. Tickets are $7.50 for adults, $3.75 for children ages three to twelve. Cruises run from April to September, weather and river conditions permitting. For cruise times and dates call (314) 621–4040. Eat on the world's only floating **McDonald's Restaurant,** which features an aquarium of river fish and a view of the river your kids will enjoy watching as they chow down.

Baseball is big in St. Louis, so if you're in town during the season, take in a game at **Busch Stadium,** 300 Stadium Plaza downtown. Tickets range from $14 for box seats to $5.50 for general admission. Call (314) 421–3060. Cardinal fans can trace the long and proud history of their team at the **St. Louis Cardinals Hall of Fame Museum,** located in the stadium. More than 100 years of baseball by some of the greatest players that ever lived can be reviewed in this small museum. Admission is $2.50 for adults, $1.50 for children ages fifteen and younger. Open daily 10:00 A.M. to 5:00 P.M. April through December and until 11:00 P.M. during stadium events. Open Monday through Friday from January through March. Stadium tours are also available. Call (314) 421–FAME.

You probably didn't realize that bowling dates back to ancient Egypt, but that's just one of the many bits of trivia you can pick up at the **National Bowling Hall of Fame and Museum,** 111 Stadium Plaza. After following some surprisingly interesting exhibits outlining the history of bowling, and seeing pictures of the greatest players of the game, you can bowl on computerized or old-fashioned lanes. Admission includes the tour and four frames of bowling and costs $5.00 for adults, $2.50 for children ages five to twelve. Open Monday through Saturday 9:00 A.M. to 5:00 P.M. and Sunday 12:00 to 5:00 P.M. April through October. Open daily 11:00 A.M. to 4:00 P.M. November through March. Call (314) 231–6340.

The **Eugene Field House and Toy Museum,** 634 South Broadway Boulevard, was the boyhood home of the famous children's poet and now is a small museum housing antique toys and dolls. Admission is $3.00 for adults, $2.00 for ages twelve through eighteen, 50 cents for ages eleven and younger. Open Wednesday through Saturday 10:00 A.M. to 4:00 P.M., Sunday 12:00 to 4:00 P.M. March through December. Open January and February by appointment only. Call (314) 421–4689.

On the south side of downtown you can stop and shop at **Soulard Market,** 730 Carroll Street, a farmer's market that has been in operation since 1779. The 150 stalls sell fruit and vegetables fresh from the farm, meat, fish, and numerous other items that change daily as merchants come and go. Open Wednesday through Friday 8:00 A.M. to 5:30 P.M. Saturdays start at 6:00 A.M. and promise the widest selection. Call (314) 622–4180.

You don't have to be a beer drinker to enjoy the **Anheuser-Busch Brewery Tour Center,** Twelfth and Lynch Streets. The free tour shows visitors the historic Clydesdale stables, a short video on the making of beer, and a bottling facility, and it ends with a short ride on a cable car and complimentary samples of beer and soft drinks. Free admission, but reservations required. Open Monday through Saturday; tours start at 9:00 A.M. and leave every forty-five minutes. Last tour leaves at 4:00 P.M. Call (314) 577–2626.

Anyone with an interest in weapons and military memorabilia will enjoy spending time at the **Soldiers' Memorial Military Museum,** 1315 Chestnut Street. This memorial to fallen soldiers has an excellent display of handheld weapons, uniforms, photos, flags, and other items, primarily from World Wars I and II, but some dating back to the Civil War. Free admission. Open daily 9:00 A.M. to 4:30 P.M. Call (314) 622–4550.

Kiel Center, 1401 Clark Avenue, regularly hosts national sporting events, concerts by national entertainers and family entertainment programs. For a schedule and ticket information call (314) 622–KIEL. In addition, the **St. Louis Blues** professional hockey team plays here from October through April. Tickets range from $30 to $55. Call (314) 622–2500. You can see the **St. Louis Ambush** professional indoor soccer team from late October to April. Tickets range from $9.00 to $15.00. Call (314) 962–4625. The **St. Louis University Billikens** basketball team also plays in this stadium. For a schedule and ticket prices call (314) 977–3182.

Tour the **Scott Joplin House State Historic Site,** 2658 Delmar Boulevard, and you can hear music written by this ragtime composer and see the house he lived in during the early part of this century. Small admission fee. Open daily 8:00 A.M. to 4:30 P.M. For information call (314) 533–1003.

While you're downtown you have to visit **Union Station,** 1820 Market Street, to shop, eat, or just see this glorious railroad station that was once one of the busiest in the world. Visit the Grand Hall, which has been restored to its original condition and is now the lobby of a luxury hotel. Pick up a self-guided tour of the station at the information booth. When you hit the shops, don't miss **The Great Train Store** for model and toy trains, **America's National Parks** with a stuffed brown bear in the window and an extensive selection of park merchandise, and **The Disney Store** where family-oriented videos are always playing. On the second level there is a food court where you can get a wide variety of fast, low-priced food. During the summer months there are regularly scheduled concerts and street performers at the station, a Ferris wheel and carousel offer rides for a small fee, and you can rent paddleboats on the man-made lake behind the station. Call (314) 421–6655.

You can enter the wonderful world of puppets at **Bob Kramer Marionette Theater,** 4143 Laclede Avenue. Master puppeteer Kramer has been practicing his craft since he was five years old. While you are there you can tour the workshop, see a one-hour demonstration of how the puppets are made, and watch a great puppet performance. The puppet shows change regularly and always include delightful seasonal productions. Tickets for a tour and show are $7.50 for adults, $6.50 for children ages two to twelve. You can also purchase tickets just for the show. For schedule or reservations call (314) 531–3313.

In the middle of town you'll find Grand Center, home to several arts organizations in St. Louis. The **Fabulous Fox** theater, 527 North Grand Boulevard, is an outrageous movie palace that has to be seen to be believed. Broadway-style shows and entertainment are offered, and you can take a tour of the theater for a small fee. For show schedule and ticket prices call (314) 534–1678. The **St. Louis Symphony,** at 718 North Grand Boulevard, offers family concerts in magnificent Powell Hall and at other locations throughout the year with summer concerts specifically for children. Call (314) 534–1700. **Dance St. Louis** performs several family programs every year, including *The Nutcracker* during the Christmas season. Call (314) 534–5000.

Forest Park, located at Kingshighway Boulevard and Highway 40, is the most popular park in the city and covers more than 1,200 acres. It is home to several of the city's finest cultural institutions and contains a scenic 7.5-mile hiking and biking trail, as well as fishing, golf, tennis, and picnic facilities. You can get around inside the park during the summer months by hopping on the Forest Park Shuttle Bug, which stops at all the park museums. Catch it at the Forest Park or Central West End Metrolink stations or one of the bus stops marked in the park. Call (314) 231–2345.

You can rent a small boat or canoe at the boathouse and fish or explore the lake. Call (314) 367–3423. You can skate at open-air **Steinberg Memorial Skating Rink.** During winter months you can ice-skate and during the summer roller skating is offered. Call (314) 361–5103. From June to August you can enjoy national entertainers and Broadway-style musicals at the **Muny** theater, the largest outdoor amphitheater in the country and a St. Louis tradition for generations. Tickets range from $6.00 to $36.00. Call (314) 361–1900.

Circus Flora, a small family circus modeled after European circuses of the nineteenth-century, performs wonderful one-ring productions that your kids will love. The up-close action is impressive to children accustomed to the anything-can-happen world of television. The circus, which tours the country throughout the year, plays in Forest Park from mid-May to mid-June. Tickets range from $8.00 to $25.00. For a schedule call (314) 531–6273.

The **History Museum,** located at the Lindell Boulevard entrance to the park, is a great midsize museum that offers information relating to the history of the city, including the 1904 St. Louis World's Fair that was held in the park, the great fire of 1849, Charles Lindbergh's Spirit of St. Louis flight over the Atlantic, African-American music, and life in the city during the Gilded Age. The exhibits are engaging enough to capture the attention of all ages and include toys, tools, clothing, and photographs from the past. Free admission. Open Tuesday through Sunday 9:30 A.M. to 5:00 P.M. Open until 8:00 P.M. on Tuesday. Call (314) 746–4599.

The **St. Louis Art Museum,** located on the highest point in the park, is the only building remaining from the fair that was held at the beginning of the century. This historic structure provides a beautiful setting for the wonderful art collection housed there. Your children will most enjoy the small Egyptian room with an authentic mummy, the period rooms of furniture, the pre-Colombian collection, and the wild twentieth-century work on the top floor. The museum offers a wide variety of educational workshops and lectures for families and children. Call for a schedule and prices. Free admission. Open Wednesday through Sunday 10:00 A.M. to 5:00 P.M., Tuesday 1:30 to 8:30 P.M. Call (314) 721–0072.

The **St. Louis Zoo** is a world-class zoo that features eighty-three acres of natural habitats housing more than 6,000 animals. Visit The Living World, a state-of-the-art education center that features interactive displays, computer games and activities, hands-on areas, and a free movie about biodiversity. Live animal exhibits are interspersed with high technology and provide close-up looks at everything from one-celled organisms to birds, fish, and mammals. It's a great opportunity to closely examine different members of the animal kingdom, but try to avoid the busiest times of the

The free St. Louis Zoo covers eighty-three acres, with most of the animals in natural, open environments. (Courtesy St. Louis Zoo)

day (from 10:00 A.M. to 3:00 P.M.) when you may have trouble getting up close to the exhibits.

The Jungle of the Apes is a natural habitat for gorillas, chimpanzees, and orangutans. The inside areas have glass enclosures that allow you to get uncomfortably close to our nearest animal relatives. Lions and tigers can be seen in Big Cat Country, nearly two acres of open-aired cages designed to match the cats' home environments. You'll also see bear pits, enclosures for hoofed animals, and a sea lion basin that date back several decades at this easy-to-navigate zoo with a long and proud heritage. A charming walk-through birdcage, the largest free-flight aviary in the world, dates from the 1904 World's Fair and houses hundreds of birds you can see up close. A new two-acre outdoor Bird Garden offers bird-watchers a natural setting with walkways, reflecting pools, and landscaped paths where they can see a large variety of bird species.

Admission to the zoo is free, but there is a small fee to take a ride on the small-scale Zooline railroad or enter the Children's Zoo, a petting area and play space. Open daily 9:00 A.M. to 5:00 P.M., Tuesday open until 8:00 P.M. during summer months. Call (314) 781–0900.

The **St. Louis Science Center,** 5050 Oakland, is a fantastic science museum that not only is great fun, but offers the added bonus of free admission. More than 500 interactive and hands-on exhibits cover such topics as the human senses, computers, flight, space, building, mining, medicine, weather, and prehistoric times. Two life-size animated dinosaurs provide a frightening touch of realism; a laser show is flashed on the wall every twenty minutes; there's an underground tunnel that simulates a coal mine; and you can shoot cars passing underneath the walkway over the highway with a radar gun to see how fast they are traveling. One gallery explores the world of modern medicine and features a continuously running video of an actual operation for those who aren't too squeamish to watch. You'll want to budget plenty of time for exploration.

The science center houses several ticketed areas, with various admission prices. A Discovery Room with exhibits specifically designed for young children offers science toys and tools to play with, a small cave and tepee to climb into, and small live animals to hold and watch. Tickets are sold for forty-five-minute sessions and cost $2.00 per person. They must be purchased the day of your visit, so get them as soon as you arrive at the center. Then you can look around while you wait for your appointment to enter the room.

A planetarium offers several shows daily featuring a look at the heavens with music and laser lights as accompaniment. Tickets for thirty-minute star shows are $3.00 for adults, $2.00 for children ages two to seventeen. More sophisticated shows with music, laser, and animation are $7.00 for adults and $6.00 for children. An Omnimax theater with a four-story-tall domed screen offers productions made specifically for the big, big screen. The theater has a 15,000-watt sound system that makes the nature and science films viewed here come alive. Tickets are $5.50 for adults, $4.50 for children ages two to seventeen. The science center is open Monday through Thursday 9:00 A.M. to 5:00 P.M., Friday 9:00 A.M. to 9:00 P.M., Saturday 10:00 A.M. to 9:00 P.M., Sunday 11:00 A.M. to 6:00 P.M. Call (314) 289–4444.

Although a visit to a church might not be your children's idea of a good time, the **Cathedral of St. Louis,** 4431 Lindell Boulevard, has the largest collection of mosaic art in the world adorning the walls and is a required stop for art lovers. A small museum in the lower level explains how mosaic art is created. Free admission to the church, open daily 8:30 A.M. to 5:00 P.M. Small fee for the museum, hours vary. Call (314) 533–0544.

The main attraction on the Hill, the Italian neighborhood at Kingshighway Boulevard and Southwest Avenue, is the food. Some of the city's finest, most expensive restaurants are here, but you can also find wonderful reasonable, family operations. Hungry families should check out **Rigazzi's Restaurant,** 4945 Daggett Avenue, where the food is plentiful and the beer is served to adults in "frozen fishbowls." Order toasted ravioli and sample the appetizer that originated on the Hill. Call (314) 772–4900. **Amigetti's Bakery,** 5141 Wilson Avenue, is famous throughout the area for great sandwiches made on the best bread in town. It's located in the heart of the Hill across from St. Ambrose, the Catholic church that has been the center of this Italian community for decades. Call (314) 776–2855.

The **Missouri Botanical Garden,** 4344 Shaw Boulevard, is one of the finest gardens in the country and promises a fascinating time. More than eighty acres are planted in a variety of gardening styles that offer something for everyone. The Climatron dominates the landscape, and all ages will enjoy seeing this geodesic dome sheltering a living tropical rain forest complete with a towering trees, a waterfall and winding paths overrun with exotic plants and greenery. There is an interactive education center about ecology and the environment as you exit the dome.

The enchanting Japanese Garden, one of the largest in North America, features graceful bridges over a lake, mini-waterfalls, giant koi fish to feed, a beautiful pebble beach, and rock stepping paths to follow. Find the Victorian maze in the back of the garden, then let your children wander at will through the confusing turns while you watch the action from atop a Victorian viewing cupola. Next to the Kemper Center for Home Gardening you'll find more than twenty demonstration gardens to give you ideas for your own backyard. A special Children's Garden combines all the fun of colorful, uniquely textured plants with topiary, rainbow colors, and unusual names to entertain and teach your children.

The Climatron, the world's first geodesic-domed garden, covers a tropical rain forest at the Missouri Botanical Garden. (Courtesy Missouri Botanical Garden)

This wonderful collection of gardens will delight your children with its scented garden of herbs to scratch and sniff, bell tower of chimes to play, sheep statuary to sit on, grass they are invited to walk on, and a fountain they can walk through for relief from the heat on summer days. Admission is $3.00 for ages thirteen to sixty-four, $1.50 for ages sixty-five and older, free for ages twelve and younger. A tram-ride tour of the gardens is available for $2.00 per person. Open daily 9:00 A.M. to 5:00 P.M. Open until 8:00 P.M. during summer months. Call (314) 577–5100.

The garden hosts several family events that are well worth the small additional fee. The **Japanese Festival,** held every year on Labor Day weekend, offers musical performances, ethnic food, cultural demonstrations and vendors selling Japanese products. The highlight of the event is the night walk through the Japanese Garden with hundreds of lanterns lining the paths and floating on the water. **Garden Expo** is held during April and features nature, gardening, and environmental activities, many geared toward children.

Just south of the garden is **Tower Grove Park,** 4255 Arsenal Street. Modeled after a Victorian walking park of the nineteenth century, it's filled with ornate gazebos and statuary and provides an excellent place for hiking or picnicking.

Going out to **Ted Drewes Frozen Custard,** 6726 Chippewa, for a "Concrete" is a St. Louis tradition you'll want to share. The frozen custard arguably is the best in the world, and the famed Concrete shakes are so thick they're served upside down to prove the point. Open March through December. Call (314) 481–2652.

The city hosts several not-to-be-missed annual events for families. The first weekend in May, the **St. Louis Storytelling Festival** offers thirty to forty professional storytellers converging from across the nation to provide free performances in various locations throughout the St. Louis area. Don't miss this delightful opportunity to experience one of the oldest performing arts in human history. Call (314) 516–6914 for times and locations. The **Great Forest Park Balloon Race** takes place in September and features thirty to fifty hot-air balloons filling the sky in a hare-and-hound race. The action starts the night before, when the balloons are tethered and lighted to create a spectacular drive-by sight, and continues the day of the race with the liftoff. Call (314) 821–6724.

For more than twenty years cyclists have been turning out in droves to participate in the **Moonlight Ramble,** an 18-mile tour held in August and starting at 2:00 A.M. downtown. Activities include safety clinics and demonstrations the evening before. Call (314) 644–4660.

The city celebrates our nation's birth with **Fair St. Louis,** one of the nation's largest birthday parties. It is held on the Arch grounds over three days and features concerts by national entertainers, air shows with aircraft from hometown company McDonnell Douglas, activity booths, ethnic foods, and small stages with performances throughout the weekend. A downtown parade starts the event, and there are fireworks every night of the fair. Call (314) 434–3434.

Families can celebrate the new year with their children at **First Night St. Louis,** held downtown beginning in the early evening on New Year's Eve. This alcohol-free celebration emphasizes arts activities for the whole family and ends after midnight with fireworks. Call (314) 664–1200.

You can travel the old-fashioned way and watch the scenery go by when you ride the rails on an Amtrak train. The St. Louis-Kansas City route takes you through the Missouri wine country and follows the Missouri River halfway across the state. There are more than a dozen stops along the way, many in charming, historic towns that offer visitors pleasant diversions on their trip. Call (800) 872–7245 or (314) 331–3300.

UNIVERSITY CITY

Just outside the St. Louis city limits sits this suburb built around Washington University and featuring many small unique stores, bars, and restaurants along Delmar Boulevard. Look for the **St. Louis Walk of Fame,** lining sidewalks on both sides of the street, with star-shaped plaques honoring famous St. Louisians and their achievements. Stop for a meal at **Fitz's Bottling Co. and Restaurant**, 6605 Delmar Boulevard, where you can see root beer being bottled while you enjoy a great meal. Call (314) 726–9555.

The Center of Contemporary Arts, a performing arts school at 524 Trinity, offers a children's theater series that is guaranteed to entertain the entire family. For a schedule of the **Frank Fowles Family Theatre Series,** call (314) 725–6555.

OVERLAND

If old cars interest you, visit the **St. Louis Car Museum,** 1575 Woodson Road. This antique car showroom usually has 150 cars on display and for sale. You can look around and if you see something you like, take it home with you. Admission is $3.75 for adults, $2.75 for children ages twelve and younger. Open Monday through Saturday 9:00 A.M. to 5:00 P.M., Sunday 11:00 A.M. to 5:00 P.M. Call (314) 993–1330.

You can't beat the hot dogs served Chicago-style at **Woofie's,** 1919 Woodson Road. Here you can get 100 percent pure beef Vienna hot dogs served with a wide variety of toppings and garnishes. Call (314) 426–6291.

CREVE COEUR

As you head west into the outer suburbs of the city, you'll find many wonderful family attractions. When the Missouri River changed course, as it frequently did in years past, it left behind an oxbow lake that now is **Creve Coeur Lake Park,** Marine and Dorsett Roads. This 1,000-acre park includes athletic fields, hiking trails, picnic and camping sites, tennis courts, and a children's playground. The 300-acre lake is open for sailing, canoeing, and fishing. Open daily 9:00 A.M. to thirty minutes after sunset. Call (314) 889–2863.

CHESTERFIELD

Farther west is **Faust Park,** 15185 Olive Street Road. This park in progress has a number of historic buildings in the process of being restored. Thornhill, the 1918 frontier home of the state's second governor, is open for tours for a small fee. The restored **St. Louis Carousel,** located in the park, was hand-carved in the 1920s. You can ride this relic from the past for a small fee. Carousel open Wednesday through Sunday 12:00 to 5:00 P.M. Park open daily 9:00 A.M. to thirty minutes after sunset. Call (314) 537–0222.

The Piwacket Children's Theater offers productions filled with rhythm, color, and songs at the Chesterfield Community Center, 16464 Burkhardt Place, from June through March. The shows feature a minimum of props and sets and are designed to spark the imaginations of children ages ten and younger. For a schedule and show times call (314) 962–9399.

When your kids need to let off steam and get physical, check out the indoor playground at the **Discovery Zone,** 14373 Manchester Road. Admission is $3.96 for toddlers ages one to three, $5.99 for children older than three. Call (314) 394–8677.

There are plenty of outdoor recreational options at **Queeny Park,** 550 Weidman Road. You'll find a recreation complex with indoor/outdoor skating rinks and a swimming pool. The park also has tennis courts, one of the best children's playgrounds in the St. Louis area, and hiking trails that wind through the more than 500 acres of parkland. Open daily 9:00 A.M. to thirty minutes after sunset. Call (314) 391–0900.

A little farther west, surrounded by subdivisions, is **Dr. Edmund A. Babler Memorial State Park,** Highway 109. The beautiful 2,400 wooded acres on the Missouri River hills encompass seventy-seven campsites, a swimming pool, a horseback-riding concession for those who don't bring their own horses, a visitor center with exhibits about native wildlife and 13 miles of hiking and equestrian trails. Call (314) 458–3813.

ELLISVILLE

The Infield, 2626 Westhills Park Drive, has something for everyone, including go-carts, an eight-stall batting cage with dual pitching machines, a miniature golf course, and an arcade with video games. Open daily 10:00 A.M. to 11:00 P.M. June through August. Call for off-season hours. Call (314) 458–1144.

GLENCOE

The **Wabash Frisco and Pacific Mini Steam Railway** leaves from here on a 2-mile round trip along the scenic Meramec River. You can catch the steam-powered miniature railroad at 109 Grand Avenue on Sunday from 12:00 to 4:20 P.M. May through October. A $2.00 donation per person is requested. For a schedule call (314) 587–3538.

BALLWIN

Castlewood State Park, 152 Kiefer Creek, is located along the Meramec River and is part of the Meramec River Recreation Area which stretches for 108 miles along the river. It's popular for canoeing and fishing and has

1,700 acres offering access to the river and 14 miles of trails for hikers, mountain bikers, and equestrians. Open daily 7:00 A.M. to 6:00 P.M. Call (314) 527–6481.

KIRKWOOD

Nature can be great fun when you learn about it at **Powder Valley Conservation Nature Center,** 11715 Cragwold Road. This center has interactive exhibits on the flora and fauna of the area. Feeding stations just outside the windows of a wonderful viewing room attract dozens of fine feathered friends and woodland wildlife. Several paved hiking trails through the surrounding wooded hills present plenty of opportunities for nature lovers to enjoy themselves. The center offers a wide range of nature programs and guided hikes for all ages. Center and trails open daily 8:00 A.M. to 6:00 P.M. Exhibits closed on Monday. Call (314) 821–8427.

Walking in the woods becomes even more enjoyable when the natural landscape is scattered with freestanding works of art, many of them specifically designed for the setting. At **Laumeier Sculpture Park,** 12580 Rott Road, you can explore more than ninety-six acres of hiking trails and woodland paths featuring modern sculpture. There also is a museum in the center of the park with indoor exhibits. Even if your children don't like art, they'll enjoy running around the park. Every August tons of sand are brought in and a fantasy sandcastle is created, weather permitting. The winter solstice is celebrated in mid-December with a fire and ice sculpture. Free admission. Park open daily 8:00 A.M. to sunset. Museum open Tuesday through Saturday 10:00 A.M. to 5:00 P.M., Sunday 12:00 to 5:00 P.M. Call (314) 821–1209.

The **National Museum of Transport,** 3015 Barrett Station Road, offers a great opportunity for train buffs of all ages. Here you can see one of the most extensive collections of locomotives and railroad cars in the country, as well as automobiles, buses, trucks, and an airplane. The collection is primarily outdoors and visitors take a self-guided tour that includes climbing into several of the locomotives and railcars. A towboat at the entrance to the museum is also fair game for climbing and exploring. A miniature train offers rides for a small fee from April through October. Admission is $4.00 for adults and children ages thirteen or older, $1.50

for children ages five to twelve. Open daily 9:00 A.M. to 5:00 P.M. year-round. Call (314) 965–7998.

If your children are school age or younger, don't miss the **Magic House,** also known as the St. Louis Children's Museum, located at 516 S. Kirkwood Road. This wonderful collection of hands-on exhibits is housed in an old three-story mansion where your children can play with water, light, or sound; experiment with pulleys and wheels; experience optical illusions; work on computers; and enjoy the slide that shoots them from the top of the house to the first floor. There is a special area for children ages one to seven where they can explore at their own pace. Admission is $3.50 for adults and children age two and older. Younger than age two are free. Open Tuesday through Saturday 9:30 A.M. to 5:30 P.M., until 9:30 P.M. on Friday. Open Sunday 11:30 A.M. to 5:30 P.M. Call (314) 822–8900.

BRENTWOOD

The **Mid-America Aquacenter,** a great aquarium that specializes in exhibits for children, is located at 416 Hanley Industrial Court. Although designed with kids in mind, all ages will enjoy the displays about the ecology of the ocean, models and exhibits of the Amazon and Mississippi Rivers, and opportunities to touch numerous aquatic creatures. The petting pool features a changing cast but usually includes an iguana, turtles, hermit crabs, and a small horned shark. There's also a pool where visitors can pet large fish. Admission is $6.95 for adults, $4.95 for children ages three to eighteen. Open daily 9:00 A.M. to 5:00 P.M. Call (314) 647–9594.

CRESTWOOD

To try your hand at indoor fun and games, visit **Exhilarama** on the lower level of Crestwood Plaza, Watson and Sappington Roads. This family arcade has video games, virtual reality games, bumper cars, and a special play space for younger children. Games are individually priced, admission to the play space for ages two to eight is $2.50. Open Monday through Friday 10:00 A.M. to 9:30 P.M., Saturday 10:00 A.M. to 11:00 P.M., Sunday 11:00 A.M. to 6:00 P.M. Call (314) 962–1134.

VALLEY PARK

Lone Elk Park is a wildlife sanctuary where you can get close to free-roaming Rocky Mountain elk, American Plains bison, white-tailed deer, wild turkeys, and other creatures. To reach the park take the service road west from the intersection of Highway 141 at Highway 44. The park has a drive-through area where the animals may come right up to your car. Other sections of the park offer picnicking and hiking trails, the longest of which is 7 miles and winds past views of the Meramec River. The Wild Bird Sanctuary operates a nature center where you can see live birds of prey being cared for and rehabilitated, and talk to rangers about conservation work. Center open daily 10:00 A.M. to 4:00 P.M. Park open 8:00 A.M. to dusk. Free admission. Call (314) 225–4390.

ALLENTON

Head a little bit to the west and you can visit one of the largest amusement parks in the Midwest, **Six Flags Over Mid-America,** Highway 44, exit 261. The park has more than 100 rides and shows in eight themed areas. In Time Warner Studios you'll find Batman The Ride, a roller coaster on which riders in ski-lift–style chairs are hurtled through loops including a zero-gravity roll. The park has two other roller coasters, the Screamin' Eagle, which roars down a three-quarter-mile wooden track at speeds up to 62 miles per hour, and the Ninja, featuring high-speed spirals, steep drops, and a double corkscrew.

The 1904 World's Fair area has a giant eighteen-story Ferris wheel that lets you survey the entire park from above; old-time cars to drive; an authentic twenty-five-ton narrow-gauge steam locomotive that provides a tour around the park; and a large theater that offers entertainment throughout the day. Several water rides promise a thorough soaking on hot summer days, and excellent shows throughout the park provide great entertainment for everyone.

Looney Tunes Town has rides for little ones too small to ride the attractions with minimum height requirements located in other areas of the park. Admission to the park is $27.95 for adults, $22.95 for children ages three to eleven. Children two and younger are free. Open daily mid-May through August. Open weekends only in fall and spring. Operating hours vary. For specific hours call (314) 938–4800.

Batman The Ride provides head-over-heels thrills at Six Flags Over Mid-America theme park.
(Courtesy Six Flags Over Mid-America)

If you plan to stay for a while, check out the **Ramada Inn at Six Flags,** adjacent to the park. There's a fundome with an indoor pool, sauna, whirlpool, and game room for unwinding after an exhausting day of having fun. Call (800) 782–8108. Camping facilities are available at **Yogi Bear's Jellystone Park Camp-Resort,** Highway 44, north on Allenton Road, then left on Fox Creek to the park entrance. In addition to RV and tent camping, there are air-conditioned cabins with kitchens, a general store, a laundromat, and outdoor recreational facilities and planned activities.

During the winter, this park is transformed into **Santa's Magical Kingdom,** a thirty-five-acre display of animated scenes, spectacular special effects, and millions of lights celebrating the holiday season. Admission is $13 per car. Open daily after dark November through December. Call (314) 938–5925.

Just to the north is **Greensfelder Park,** Allenton and Hencken Roads, with 1,700 wooded acres offering picnic shelters, children's playground, and miles of nature trails for hikers, mountain bikers, and horse-

back riders. Open daily 9:00 A.M. to thirty minutes after sunset. Call
(314) 889–2863. **Rockwoods Reservation,** Highway 109 and Manchester Road, is a 1,900-acre forest and wildlife preserve that offers seven easy
hiking-only trails through beautiful, unspoiled land. Start at the visitor center and pick up maps and brochures about the area and information about
nature activities. There's a touch table with natural artifacts for curious little fingers. Center open daily 8:00 A.M. to 5:00 P.M. Area open from sunrise
to half an hour after sunset. Call (314) 458–5006.

Skiing enthusiasts can try their skill at **Hidden Valley Ski Resort,**
17409 Hidden Valley Drive, which has eight ski trails, two chairlifts,
four rope tows, and a ski lodge. Season runs from December through
March with man-made snow providing continuous snow coverage. Call
(314) 938–5373.

The **Wolf Sanctuary** at Tyson Research Center, Highway 44, west
off exit 269, houses four species of endangered wolves and offers tours of
the facility and special programs. Evening programs include campfire storytelling and howling exhibitions. You can get a one-hour tour of the center
for $5.00 per person. Admission by appointment only. For a schedule of
events call (314) 938–5900.

GRAY SUMMIT

Animal lovers should definitely plan a stop at **Purina Farms,** the free visitor center operated by Ralston Purina Company and Purina Mills, Inc. To
reach the farm take Highway 44, then go north on Highway 100 and left
on County Road MM to the entrance 1 mile on the left. This attraction features interesting educational displays, videos and hands-on activities about
the role domestic animals play in our lives. Several buildings house live animals for petting, including horses, cows, sheep, pigs, goats, chickens, and
ducks. Smaller animals are in petting corrals that encourage visitors to get
close and friendly. The cats and dogs have their own special house where
you can see a variety of breeds.

A hayloft equipped with ropes for swinging and hay bales for climbing
provides the perfect play space for children. Special events are planned
around holidays, and an outdoor theater hosts animal demonstrations and
shows. Free admission, but reservations are required. Open Tuesday

through Sunday 9:30 A.M. to 3:00 P.M. Memorial Day through Labor Day. For spring and fall hours, or to make reservations, call (314) 982–3232.

Shaw Arboretum and Nature Reserve, Highway 100, is one of the best places in this region for nature walks. The 2,400-acre preserve has 14 miles of hiking trails that pass oak-hickory forest, meadows, a flood-plain, limestone bluffs, and the Meramec River. A four-acre wildflower garden, 100 acres of tallgrass prairie, a gravel bar on the river, and a boardwalk trail over wetlands provide a wide range of environments to see. The Manor House is an interpretive center that has exhibits on human land use and the various ways man relates to his environment. Admission is $3.00 for adults; children ages twelve and younger are free. The area is open daily 7:00 A.M. to thirty minutes after sunset. Center open Monday through Friday 8:00 A.M. to 4:30 P.M., Saturday and Sunday 9:00 A.M. to 5:00 P.M. Call (314) 742–3512.

AFFTON

In the southern suburbs of the city, you can visit a wonderfully relaxed and delightful minizoo called **Grant's Farm,** 10501 Gravois Road. This free attraction is run by the Anheuser-Busch Company and is located on the grounds of the Busch family's ancestral home. There is a petting zoo where you can hand-feed some of the animals, and several animal shows are offered. In the Bauernhof courtyard you'll find stables housing several Clydesdale horses as well as the family's collection of equestrian equipment and trophies. In this area visitors over the age of twenty-one can obtain a free sample of the company's products, or you can purchase soft drinks and snacks.

Your visit to the park ends with a twenty-minute ride through Deer Park, a nature preserve with more than thirty kinds of animals roaming freely. You'll also pass the historic cabin built by Ulysses S. Grant, for whom the property is named. If you love the Clydesdales, don't miss the stallion barn at the north edge of the parking lot, where you can see several breeders in their home stalls. Free admission, but reservations are required. Open Tuesday through Sunday 9:00 A.M. to 3:15 P.M. June through August. Open Thursday through Sunday 9:00 A.M. to 3:15 P.M. during April, May, September and October. Call (314) 843–1700.

Right next door to Grant's Farm is the **Ulysses S. Grant National Historic Site,** 7400 Grant Road. This property, known as White Haven, was originally the family plantation of Grant's wife, Julia Dent. There are five historic buildings on the ten-acre site, including a two-story residence. Park rangers offer tours through the family home and programs about the Grants and the time period in which they lived. Hours vary due to ongoing historic renovation work. Free admission. Open daily 9:00 A.M. to 5:00 P.M. Call (314) 842–3298.

At **Jefferson Barracks Historic Park,** 533 Grant Road, you can learn about the U.S. military from the early 1800s to World War II. In the park are two museums devoted to the proud military history of this installation, which operated for more than 170 years and housed some of the greatest soldiers of our country. The park also has several ideal overlooks of the Mississippi River, as well as picnic areas, archery fields, and bike and hiking trails. The National Association of Civilian Conservation Corps Alumni has its national headquarters in the park and also operates a museum here. A National Cemetery is adjacent to the historic park. Free admission, except during special events. The park is open from sunup to thirty minutes after sunset. For hours for each of the museums call (314) 544–5714.

Learn about the history and lore of the rivers, and the steamboats that plied those waterways, at the **Golden Eagle River Museum** in **Bee Tree Park,** Finestown and Becker Roads. This small museum has boat models, pictures, artifacts, and memorabilia housed in a mansion perched on picturesque bluffs that provide a commanding view of the Mississippi River. Free admission. Open Wednesday to Sunday 1:00 to 5:00 P.M. May through October. Call (314) 846–9073. The park has fishing spots, hiking trails, picnic shelters, and a children's playground. Park open daily 9:00 A.M. to thirty minutes after sunset.

MEHLVILLE

At **Springdale Pool and Miniature Golf,** 2280 South Highway 141, you'll find an enormous swimming pool, picnic grounds, and a miniature golf course. Every October the park turns into **Halloween Doom's Day,** a 2,000-square-foot walk-through horror show that includes both indoor and outdoor exhibits and promises the fright of your life. Recommended for ages eight and older. Call (314) 343–2123.

JANE'S TOP ANNUAL EVENTS IN THE NORTHEAST REGION

St. Patrick's Day Parades, March, St. Louis, (800) 325–7962 or (314) 421–1023

Lewis and Clark Rendezvous, third weekend in May, St. Charles, (800) 366–2427 or (314) 946–7776

St. Louis Storytelling Festival, May, St. Louis, (314) 553–5911

Fair St. Louis, Fourth of July weekend, St. Louis, (314) 434–3434

National Tom Sawyer Days, Fourth of July weekend, Hannibal, (573) 221–2477

Japanese Festival, Labor Day weekend, Missouri Botanical Gardens, St. Louis, (314) 577–5100

Haunted Forest, October, Tilles Park, St. Louis County, (314) 889–2458

Winter Wonderland Light Display, mid-November through end of December, Tilles Park, St. Louis County, (314) 889–2863

Don't miss the farm area at **Suson Park,** Wells Road south of Highway 21, where you can see barnyard animals such as ducks, geese, chickens, cows, goats, horses, and donkeys. The three barns are open 10:00 A.M. to 3:00 P.M. daily from April through October and on weekends from November through March. In the park you'll find picnic tables, a children's playground, and three small lakes for fishing. Call (314) 889–2863.

IMPERIAL

You can see the place where humans and mastodons were first discovered together at **Mastodon State Historic Site,** 1551 Seckman Road. Known as the Kimmswick Bonebeds, this site is where the first evidence that mastodons and ice-age people lived at the same time was unearthed. A museum displays a life-size mastodon skeleton replica and ancient artifacts excavated from the area. It also features a diorama and exhibits explaining the end of the last ice age and a twelve-minute slide show about the site. The 400-acre site is ideal for hikes and picnics. Admission is $2.00 for adults; children ages fourteen and younger are free. Museum open Monday through Saturday 9:00 A.M. to 4:30 P.M., Sunday 12:00 to 4:30 P.M. Call (314) 464–2976.

KIMMSWICK

This tiny town south of the St. Louis suburban area is often called a living museum. Start your visit at the **Kimmswick Visitors Center,** 314 Market Street. Here you can see photos and displays of the town's history and pick up maps and information about shops and restaurants in the area. Open Tuesday through Friday 10:00 A.M. to 4:00 P.M., Saturday and Sunday 10:30 A.M. to 5:00 P.M. Call (314) 464–6464. As you walk along the streets you'll feel as if you have stepped back in time and will find many small, unusual craft shops and stores. The **Apple Butter Festival,** held the end of October, is a good time to visit, but expect to encounter crowds. There are demonstrations of pioneer skills like broom making, candle making, and blacksmithing, as well as a craft show, food booths, and a wide range of musical performances. All shops and restaurants are closed on Monday.

DESOTO

Nestled in the forest is **Washington State Park,** Highway 21, once a ceremonial burial ground for prehistoric native people. Today you can see the petroglyphs, or rock carvings, they left behind near the southern boundary of the park. Big River, a tributary of the Meramec River, borders the park and provides wonderful opportunities for recreation. You can rent a canoe at the park and arrange to float from 3 to 22 miles. Tubing is a favorite activity on this small, shallow river, and the inner tubes can also be rented at the park. Kitchen-equipped cabins and campsites are available in the park, as well as a lodge that is open from April through October. An interpretive center provides information and activities throughout the summer. Call (314) 586–2995. For cabin reservations call (314) 586–0322.

Southeast Region

Missouri's southeast region is almost completely rural, but it offers incredible outdoor recreational opportunities and many revealing insights into the past. The federal government is one of the biggest landowners, with jurisdiction over the Mark Twain National Forest, much of which is located in this region, and the Ozark National Scenic Riverways. The Mark Twain National Forest has more than 1.5 million acres of some of the most remote terrain in the state. The federally supervised forest and riverways offer visitors a beautiful, unspoiled natural environment to explore freely. Small historic towns dot the countryside and reveal the rich heritage of this area.

STE. GENEVIEVE

This delightful historic town was the first permanent settlement west of the Mississippi River and promises tourists of all ages a great time. Start at the **Great River Road Interpretive Center,** 66 South Main Street. After you view the exhibits about the river, watch a film, and pick up information about the area, you can walk to many of the historic buildings and homes. Free admission. Open daily 9:00 A.M. to 4:00 P.M. Call (800) 373–7007 or (573) 883–7097.

For information about the city's history, visit the **Ste. Genevieve Museum,** next to the visitor center. Many of the religious artifacts, such as vestments, crucifixes, and relics, demonstrate the importance of the Roman Catholic Church in this French town. Small admission charge. Open daily

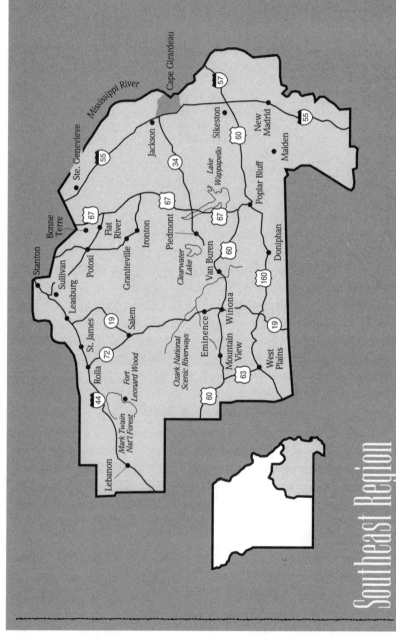

Southeast Region

9:00 A.M. to 4:00 P.M. April through October, and 12:00 to 4:00 P.M. the rest of the year. Call (573) 883–3461.

The historic buildings in this town represent three different time periods in the history of this area: the early French settlers, the Americans who came during the early 1800s, and the German immigrants who came later. You and your children might enjoy discussing the differences. You can tour the **Felix Valle House State Historic Site,** Merchant and Second Streets; the **Bolduc House,** 125 South Main; the **Maison Guibourd Valle,** 1 North Fourth Street; and the **Guibourd-Valle House,** Fourth and Merchant. Small admission fee for each house. Hours vary, so call the visitor center before you visit.

If dressing up and playing make-believe is your family's idea of a good time, check out the **Steiger Haus Bed and Breakfast Inn,** 1021 Market Street. The owners concoct elaborate storylines and stage murder mystery weekends for their guests. It's great fun and they have G-rated mysteries for family groups. Your identity for the weekend is mailed to you in advance so you can plan your costumes, and then the mystery is enacted during dinner at a local hotel and throughout the weekend. It's a weekend your family won't soon forget. Call (573) 883–5881.

The **Fête de Jour,** held the second weekend in August, has parades, folk dances, and live entertainment. It's also one of the largest crafts fairs in the state, with exhibitors coming from all over the Midwest. Call (800) 373–7007 or (573) 883–7097.

You may notice that this downtown is no longer on the riverfront because the river changed course years ago. But you can still get to the river by stopping at the **Marina de Gabouri,** located off Marina Avenue. You can watch the river traffic while you eat at the **Eagle's Nest** restaurant, and boaters who want to explore the river below the lock and dam system can access the river here. Call (573) 883–5599.

You can take your car and family across the river and visit historic sites on the Illinois side. The **Ste. Genevieve-Modoc Ferry,** operates Monday to Saturday 6:00 A.M. to 6:00 P.M., Sunday 9:00 A.M. to 6:00 P.M., river and weather conditions permitting. To reach the ferry take Main Street north from downtown to the river. Call (573) 883–7415.

Hawn State Park, Highway 144, is one of the most beautiful parks in the state. The 4,800-acre preserve has native pines, hardwoods, and numerous dogwoods, redbuds, and wild azaleas. A 10-mile hiking trail takes you to Pickle Creek and the River Aux Vases. Picnicking and camping facilities are available; naturalists offer guided hikes and programs in the summer. Call (573) 883–3603.

JACKSON

The **St. Louis Iron Mountain and Southern Railway,** Highways 61 and 25, is a two-hour amusement ride into the past. You board authentic passenger cars from the 1920s and set off pulled by a steam locomotive. Then the fun begins. There's always plenty of excitement on board, from visits by members of the Jesse James Gang, to strolling magicians and even a murder during a special four-hour trip. The steam engine runs Wednesday, Friday, Saturday, and Sunday April through October. A diesel engine runs on Saturday November through March. Day and dinner tours available. Call (800) 455–RAIL or (573) 243–1688.

Visitors to **Bollinger Mill State Historic Site,** Highway HH, also step back in time, on a forty-five-minute tour of this five-story operating mill. In addition to the tour, there are exhibits about the history of the mill. Next to the mill is a covered bridge where outdoor exhibits explain the role of covered bridges in the state. Small fee for tours. Open Monday through Saturday 9:00 A.M. to 4:00 P.M., Sunday 12:00 to 4:00 P.M. Call (573) 243–4591.

CAPE GIRARDEAU

Take a drive around the downtown area of this college town to see eight murals depicting the heritage of the area. Pick up a map or get information about attractions in the area at the Convention and Visitors Bureau, 2121 Broadway. Open Monday through Friday 8:00 A.M. to 5:00 P.M. Call (800) 777–0068 or (573) 335–1631. A scenic view of the river can be found at **Cape Rock Park,** an overlook area reached by taking Main Street until it ends, then turning right and driving for several miles directly to the park.

The **Cape River Heritage Museum,** 538 Independence Street, has exhibits about the town's history in an old building downtown that once housed the city hall and the fire and police stations. A full-size fire engine is among the hands-on displays for children. Small admission fee. Open

The St. Louis Iron Mountain and Southern Railway features one of the few remaining operating steam locomotives.

Wednesday, Friday, and Saturday 11:00 A.M. to 4:00 P.M. March through December. Call (573) 334–0405.

Southeast Missouri State University is located between Henderson Avenue and Pacific Street in the central part of the city. Walk around the campus and visit the free **University Museum,** which has historical exhibits and displays artwork by regional artists. Hours vary, so call before you visit. Call (573) 651–2260.

The **Show Me Center** on campus offers a full schedule of performances and productions, from concerts by national musicians and groups, to rodeos, children's shows, and musicals. For ticket prices and a schedule call (573) 651–2297.

Trail of Tears State Park, Highway 177, is a 3,600-acre park along the river with towering limestone bluffs and hillsides covered with mixed hardwood forests. A visitor center explains the region's natural history, as well as the tragic story of the Cherokee Indians' forced march through this area. There are photographs, maps, and memorabilia, as well as a video presentation. Open daily 9:00 A.M. to 5:00 P.M. April through October. Closed Monday and Tuesday from November through March. The park also has picnic areas, campsites, hiking trails overlooking the river, and a lake with a boat ramp and a sand beach. Call (573) 334–1711.

SIKESTON

The original **Lambert's Cafe: Home of Throwed Rolls,** 2515 East Malone Street, promises a great meal and an entertaining time. During your meal, fresh-baked rolls are thrown to you and you can choose from "pass arounds," side dishes that change daily and are provided free of charge. Expect huge portions, a menu with an extensive selection, and reasonable prices. Open daily 10:30 A.M. to 9:30 P.M. Call (573) 471–4261.

People come from all over the Midwest to attend the state's largest rodeo, and contenders come from all over the United States to compete for $80,000 in prize money at the **Sikeston Bootheel Rodeo,** held every year in August at the Rodeo Grounds north of town. The big event for this part of the state features big-name entertainers, some of the top cowboys in the country, clowns, horse competitions, roping events, and bullfights. Tickets range from $12 to $18, with alcohol-free seating available. Call (800) 455–BULL.

For a scenic drive into the delta area of the state, take I–55 south of town, turn east on Highway 80, then proceed south on Highway 77 to the **Towasahgy State Historic Site.** Here you can see the remains of a fortified Indian village from the Mississippian Culture. Then head west to Highway 102 and follow it south to **Big Oak Tree State Park,** which covers more than 1,000 acres and features majestic trees towering over the rich delta area. A boardwalk through the park lets you see the remnants of the vast swamp forest that once covered this part of the state. There are picnic areas, shelters, and a small lake for fishing. Call (573) 649–3149.

NEW MADRID

Called New *Mad*-rid by locals, this small town has an unsettling reputation. Sitting on a major fault line, it is the site of the country's worst earthquake in the nineteenth century. Visit the **New Madrid Historical Museum,** 1 Main Street, and view exhibits about earthquakes and the Civil War. Small admission fee. Open Monday through Saturday 9:00 A.M. to 4:00 P.M., Sunday 12:00 to 4:00 P.M. Call (573) 748–5944. Visit the opulent **Hunter-Dawson Home State Historic Site,** Highway U, and see how the southern gentry in this part of the state lived before the Civil War. Admission is $2.00 for adults, $1.25 for children ages six to twelve; ages five and younger are free. Open daily. Call (573) 748–5340.

If you want to give your kids a look at the Mississippi, take Main Street south to the levee, where an observation deck that juts into the river affords an 8-mile view. A **Missouri Tourist Information Center,** Highway 55, can provide you with all the information you want about attractions in this area or anywhere else in the state. Call (573) 643–2654.

MALDEN

Heading west you'll find the **Bootheel Youth Museum,** 700 A North Douglas Road. But don't be misled by the name: this hands-on, interactive discovery place will delight children of all ages. In 10,000 square feet of display space, kids can climb on a 1927 fire truck and wear a real firefighter's uniform, see a seismograph monitoring earthquake activity, simulate an earthquake on a computer, build structures with huge plastic blocks, create life-size shadows in the shadow room, and shop in a kid-size grocery store. Admission is $2.50 per person. Open Monday through Friday 10:00 A.M. to 4:00 P.M., Saturday 10:00 A.M. to 5:00 P.M., Sunday 1:00 to 5:00 P.M. May through August. Open weekends only in fall, winter, and spring. Call (573) 276–3600.

POPLAR BLUFF

If you drive to the northwest you'll enter the beautiful foothills of the Ozark Mountains. In the small town of Poplar Bluff you'll find the **Poplar Bluff Railroad Museum,** 303 Moran Street, with railroad memorabilia displayed in an old depot. Free admission. For hours call (573) 785–4539. You can tour an extensive personal collection of travel memorabilia at the **Epps-Houts Memorial Museum,** off Highway PP. This private museum is filled with items from Korea, Saudi Arabia, Iran, and

JANE'S TOP FAMILY ADVENTURES IN THE SOUTHEAST REGION

1. St. Louis Iron Mountain and Southern Railway, Jackson, (800) 455–RAIL or (573) 243–1688
2. Mark Twain National Forest, (573) 783–7225
3. Wappapello Lake, (573) 297–3247
4. Elephant Rocks State Park, Graniteville, (573) 546–3454
5. Johnson Shut-Ins State Park, south of Graniteville, (573) 546–2450
6. Bonne Terre Mine, Bonne Terre, (573) 358–2148
7. Current and Jack's Fork Rivers, (573) 729–7700
8. Eleven Point River, (573) 325–4233

Africa purchased by the owners during thirty-five years spent traveling around the world. The museum is open by appointment only, with admission ranging from $2.00 to $5.00 depending on the length of the tour. Call (573) 785–2734.

More than 27,000 acres of bottomland forests and cypress swamp have been preserved at **Mingo National Wildlife Refuge** and **Duck Creek Wildlife Area.** These two areas are rich in wildlife and offer beautiful hiking trails through natural areas. At Mingo you'll find a 1-mile boardwalk trail where you can see muskrat, beaver, wood ducks, tree frogs, turtles, watersnakes, woodpeckers, and songbirds. Observation towers in several locations provide a panoramic view of the marsh. On Sundays in April, October, and November, you can go on a 25-mile auto tour featuring glimpses of deer, raccoons, wild turkeys, owls, and hawks. At Duck Creek, visit Pool 1 to see waterfowl from October through March, and bald eagles year-round. To reach the areas take Highway 60 east, then go north on Highway 51 to the area entrance. Stop at the visitor center for information and directions. Call (573) 222–3589.

LAKE WAPPAPELLO

This 8,500-acre lake is surrounded by large tracts of public land and undeveloped areas. Because it is a shallow lake, it is not as popular with powerboaters as other lakes in the state. But it offers great fishing, sailing, and swimming areas in a natural, unspoiled state. Several national trails, including the Ozark Trail, pass through this area. **Lake Wappapello State Park,** Highway 172, located at the southern end of the lake, has eighty campsites, several housekeeping cabins, a 150-foot sand beach, and a fully equipped marina. A 15-mile trail is available for hiking, backpacking, and all-terrain bicycling, and a shorter trail provides wonderful lake views. Call (573) 297–3247.

PIEDMONT

Just west of this town is **Clearwater Lake,** a gorgeous 1,600-acre lake in a wilderness setting. Although the area is primarily rural, there are numerous resorts, campgrounds, and marinas to provide boating, swimming, skiing, and fishing throughout the lake area. Canoeing is available on the Black River north of the lake. A visitor center at the dam, Highway HH, provides information about five public recreation areas on the lake and gives you directions to beautiful Lon Sanders Canyon, a narrow rocky gorge that is worth a visit. Open Friday through Monday 9:00 A.M. to 4:00 P.M. Memorial Day through Labor Day. Call (800) 818–4046 or (573) 223–7777.

Sam A. Baker State Park, Highway 143, is northeast of the lake in the St. Francois Mountains, one of the most ancient ranges in North America geologically speaking. More than 5,000 wilderness acres surround Mudlick Mountain, with a 15-mile trail providing access to the mountain. The park has a dining lodge, cabins, more than 200 campsites, and a clear stream for swimming. A nature center has exhibits about this mountain area. Call (573) 856–4223.

Farther north is the highest point in the state, at **Taum Sauk Mountain State Park,** Highway CC. This rugged park covers more than 6,000 acres and has picnic grounds, primitive campsites, and a paved hiking path to the high point. Call (573) 546–2450.

When you're in this area don't leave without visiting the incredible **Johnson's Shut-Ins State Park,** Highway N, where the swift Black River runs around huge exposed boulders to create gorges, or "shut-ins." The result is a series of pools, chutes, and waterfalls that form a kind of natural water park. If you want your children to learn to appreciate the joys of nature, this is the place to bring them. The 8,500-acre park has campsites, picnic areas, and hiking trails and is primarily wilderness area. Call (573) 546–2450.

The park is a major trailhead for the **Ozark Trail,** which winds through Missouri and Arkansas in some of the remotest areas of the Ozark Mountains. For trail information and maps call (800) 334–6946.

IRONTON

Civil War buffs won't want to bypass **Fort Davidson State Historic Site,** north of town on Highway V. Remnants of the bloody battlefield's earthworks are still visible in this thirty-seven-acre park. There are picnic areas and a small museum with exhibits that use fiber optics to demonstrate the troop movements during the battle, and you can go on a self-guided walking tour of the battlefield. Free admission. Open Monday through Saturday 10:00 A.M. to 4:00 P.M., Sunday 12:00 to 5:00 P.M. Call (573) 546–3454.

This district of the **Mark Twain National Forest** has four recreational areas with campsites, picnic areas, and hiking trails in beautiful, secluded wilderness. At the Silver Mines Recreation Area, the trails offer magnificent views of the St. Francis River and the bluffs and shut-ins along the river. To reach the area take Highway 72, then turn south on Highway D. Call (573) 783–7225.

GRANITEVILLE

Elephant Rocks State Park, Highway 21, lives up to its name with giant granite boulders a billion years old standing end to end. Follow a trail through the rocks and see Dumbo, the largest of the rocks at twenty-seven feet tall and thirty-five feet long. Picnic grounds and a fishing lake are also available. Call (573) 546–3454.

FLAT RIVER

This area to the north was lead-mining country in the last century, and the remains of that industry now provide recreation for tourists. **St. Joe State Park,** 2800 Pimville Road, is the second-largest park in the state system and has 1,600 acres designated for off-road vehicles. During the mining process, pulverized limestone was dumped throughout the area, creating acres of sandflats that are now open for motorcycles, dune buggies, and four-wheel-drive vehicles. The entire park covers more than 8,000 acres and includes campsites, horseback-riding and hiking trails, picnic areas, and four clear lakes, two with sand beaches. Call (573) 431–1069.

The hulking mining complex of the company that worked this area has been preserved and maintained as the **Missouri Mines State Historic Site,** located in the park. In the powerhouse building are three galleries with pieces of restored mining equipment and exhibits on geology and mineral resources. You'll feel like you've entered a ghost town as you drive around this old mining facility comprising twenty-eight separate structures. Small admission fee. Open Monday through Saturday 10:00 A.M. to 4:00 P.M., Sunday 12:00 to 5:00 P.M. Call (573) 431–6226.

BONNE TERRE

Tours of the **Bonne Terre Mine,** Highways 67 and 47, lead into the bowels of the earth and through an 80-square-mile man-made cavern created during more than 100 years of mining. When the mine closed and the pumps were shut off, the underground area filled up with water and is now used by diving enthusiasts. The walking tour is $9.50 for adults, $5.00 for children ages five to eleven. A pontoon boat tour is $15 for all ages. Open daily 9:00 A.M. to 5:00 P.M. April through October. Open Friday, Saturday, and Sunday from November through March. Call (573) 358–2148.

Pick your own produce at **Eckert's Country Store and Farms,** Highway K, during the harvest season for strawberries, peaches, raspberries, apples, pumpkins, and mums. In October there's a family fun fest with wagon rides and country music. Before you go, call the hotline to find out about crop-ripening dates. Call (573) 358–5615.

POTOSI

This district of the Mark Twain National Forest has more than 100 miles of hiking trails through a variety of Ozark topographies. The highly developed Council Bluff Recreation Area surrounds a lake with a sand beach and has campsites, picnic areas, and several boat launch sites. Primitive camping is available along the Ozark Trail, which runs through this district. Call (573) 438–5427.

Families that demand a physically active vacation can find what they need at **Trout Lodge,** Route 2. Run by the YMCA, this family resort offers lodge rooms and private cabins with all meals, facilities, and most activities included in the price of the room. Activities include tennis, sailing, archery, fishing, volleyball, canoeing, and soccer. A complete fitness center, movies, campfires, and stocked ponds are also available. Prices range from $77 to $102 per night for adults; prices for kids are $38 for ages fourteen and older, $24 for ages three to thirteen. Call (573) 438–2154 or (314) 942–4002.

SULLIVAN

Northwest of the lead-mining area is **Meramec State Park,** Highway 185, along the scenic banks of the Meramec River. This 6,700-acre park has rugged forested hills, river bluffs, several springs, and more than thirty caves. A dining lodge, 200 campsites, cabins, canoe rentals, and a motel also are available. Nature programs are offered year-round and the visitor center includes a 3,500-gallon aquarium and life-size diorama. Ninety-minute guided tours through **Fisher Cave** with handheld lights are available for a fee April through October. Call (573) 468–6072.

STANTON

You won't want to miss **Meramec Caverns,** Highway 44, exit 230. This incredible cave has been attracting tourists since 1935 and is one of the most popular in the state. Guided tours last approximately eighty minutes. The guides explain geologic and historical aspects of the cave and even point out the hideout site of outlaw Jesse James. Admission is $10.00 for adults, $5.00 for children ages five to eleven; ages four and younger are free. Open daily 9:00 A.M. to 4:00 P.M., until 7:00 P.M. during spring, summer, and fall. Call (573) 468–CAVE. A motel, camp-

JANE'S TOP ANNUAL EVENTS IN THE SOUTHEAST REGION

Bluegrass Music Festival, July, Sam A. Baker State Park,
   (573) 856–4223
Fâte de Jour, second weekend in August, Ste. Genevieve,
   (800) 373–7007 or (573) 883–7097
Sikeston Bootheel Rodeo, August, Sikeston, (800) 455–BULL or
   (573) 471–2498
SEMO District Fair, September, Cape Girardeau, (800)
   777–0068 or (573) 335–1631
Current River Days, first weekend in October, Van Buren,
   (800) OZARKVB

grounds, a gift shop, and scenic boat rides are available at the cave during the summer.

If you're fascinated by the notorious James Gang, stop in the **Jesse James Wax Museum,** Highway 44, exit 230, and see them modeled in wax and set in life-size dioramas. The museum also includes an extensive collection of guns and dolls. Admission is $3.00 for adults, $1.00 for children ages six to eleven. Open daily 9:00 A.M. to 6:00 P.M. Call (573) 927–5233.

LEASBURG

If you can tour only one cave in this region, **Onondaga Cave,** located in **Onondaga Cave State Park,** Highway H, is your best bet, since it is one of the most outstanding caves in the country. A visitor center has exhibits about the cave's ecosystem and seventy-five-minute guided tours teach about the cave formations and the wildlife living inside the cave. Admission is $7.00 for adults, $5.00 for children ages thirteen to nineteen, $3.00 for ages six to twelve. Open daily 9:00 A.M. to 5:00 P.M. March through October. Call (573) 245–6600. Guided tours using handheld lights are available at **Cathedral Cave,** also located in the park. This tour is much more strenuous, with a quarter-mile hike to the cave entrance, and is available on weekends only.

The 1,300-acre park has seventy-two campsites; 3 miles of hiking trails; and swimming, canoeing, and fishing areas on the Meramec River. Call (573) 245–6576.

ST. JAMES

This small town to the southwest features **Maramec Spring Park,** Highway 8, a private park with campsites, picnic areas, a playground, a restaurant, hiking trails, a trout-fishing stream, and three museums. The park is the site of the first ironworks west of the Mississippi River and a walking trail takes you through the remnants of the mining community. A $2.00 per car admission fee to the park covers entry to the museums. Open daily during the daylight hours. Call (573) 265–7124.

ROLLA

This city is the home of the **University of Missouri–Rolla** campus, the state's principal engineering school. The university was once known as the Missouri School of Mines, and the free **Mineral Museum,** 125 McNutt Hall, chronicles that past with mineral specimens from all over the world. For hours call (573) 341–4616. A partial replica of Stonehenge sits at Fourteenth Street and Bishop Avenue. For a tour of the campus, go to the admissions office in Parker Hall or call (573) 341–4164.

Historic items from all over the county are on display at the free **Phelps County Museum,** Third and Main Streets. You'll find Civil War items recovered from a nearby fort of that time, Indian projectile points dating back hundreds of years, and many photographs from the past. Open Sunday 1:00 to 4:00 P.M. Call (573) 341–4874.

At **Memoryville USA,** Highway 63 North, you can literally stroll down memory lane on a re-creation of the city's main street at the turn of the century. A collection of sixty antique and classic automobiles can be viewed, and the site also has an art gallery and gift shop. Admission is $2.75 for adults, $1.25 for children ages seven to twelve; ages six and younger are free. Call (573) 364–1810.

The hiking trails in this district of the Mark Twain National Forest offer a unique variety of landscapes, with rivers, creeks, hills, and one of the most spectacular collapsed caves in the state. Horseback-riding trails, campsites, and a stocked river are also available. Call (573) 364–4501.

SALEM

This town to the south is the gateway to some of the most beautiful natural areas in the country. **Dillard Mill State Historic Site,** northeast of town on Highway 49, is at the junction of Indian and Huzzah creeks. It features spring-fed creeks, a rock dam, and a waterfall cascading into a millpond in one of the most picturesque settings in the state. Tours of the operational mill are available for a small fee. Open Monday to Saturday 10:00 A.M. to 4:00 P.M., Sunday 11:00 A.M. to 5:00 P.M. There are picnic areas and hiking trails in the park. Call (573) 244–3120. The Huzzah Creek is a favorite float stream, and you'll find many canoe outfitters and campgrounds in this area and to the north.

South of town are the **Ozark National Scenic Riverways,** a national treasure. More than 130 miles of shoreline along the banks of the Current and Jack's Fork Rivers is managed by the National Park Service and open to the public for swimming, camping, canoeing, rafting, and enjoying nature. This is Big Springs country, with the world's largest concentration of natural springs. From this area to the Arkansas border you'll find numerous clear, fast-running, spring-fed streams offering superb scenery and numerous opportunities for outdoor recreation. You can camp on gravel bars along the rivers or in established campsites at numerous points along the rivers.

The area also has countless outfitters ready to rent you a canoe or raft. During summer months the streams turn into "canoe highways" filled with floaters. But don't shy away for fear of crowds; floating on an Ozark stream lined with limestone bluffs and lush forests is an experience not to be missed. If you go during the week, you may have the stream all to yourself. Another way to avoid crowds is to float during the spring or fall, but be aware that these spring-fed streams have extremely cold water. Call for flooding information before you go during either of these seasons.

The streams in this area are Class I and II, meaning they provide an easy float and are suitable for novices and families with children. Visit the

Canoeing is a favorite activity on the rugged, unspoiled Jack's Fork River, part of the Ozark National Scenic Riverways. (Courtesy Missouri Division of Tourism)

Ozark Information Center, 702 South Main Street, to get information about the area. Open Monday through Sunday 9:00 A.M. to 5:00 P.M. Memorial Day through Labor Day. Call (573) 729–7700.

Highway 19, running north and south in this area, also provides sensational scenery as it crosses three streams and passes through the national forest.

Be sure to visit **Montauk State Park,** Highway 119, where Montauk Springs and Pigeon Creek form the headwaters of the **Current River.** The park has an old gristmill you can tour and 1,300 acres with 200 campsites, a motel, 52 housekeeping cabins, and a modern lodge. The stream is stocked with rainbow trout and attracts fisherman during the season from March through October. Call (800) 334–6946 or (573) 548–2201.

The northernmost access to the Current River is just southeast of the park. When traveling by river on the upper Current, you can see Cave Spring, where you paddle inside the cave for approximately 100 feet; Welch Spring and the ruins of a nineteenth-century hospital; and historic

Akers Ferry, which takes visitors across the river. The ferry operates daily 7:00 A.M. to 9:00 P.M. during the summer months. Reduced hours during fall, spring, and winter. Call (573) 858–3224. The beautiful, aquamarine **Round Spring,** Highway 19, can be accessed by water or land. A cave on the site can be explored with handheld lights during an hour-long tour. There is an admission fee for the tour of the cave, which is open from Memorial Day to Labor Day. Call (573) 323–4236.

EMINENCE

This town lies close to the junction of the Current and the **Jack's Fork River,** which starts near the tiny town of Mountain View to the west. On this part of the Jack's Fork River you'll find **Alley Spring** and the three-story **Alley Spring Grist Mill,** which is a museum. This area of the river-way has hiking trails, a one-room schoolhouse open to the public, campsites, and swimming and picnic areas. Call (573) 323–4236.

WINONA

This district of the **Mark Twain National Forest** is traversed by the Eleven Point and Current Rivers and is particularly popular for water recre-ation. The **Eleven Point River,** one of the most scenic rivers in the state, is part of the National Wild and Scenic River System, which aims at pre-serving rivers in their natural state. Greer Spring, located off Highway 19, is a 1-mile hike from the highway parking lot. Benches along the path pro-vide rest stops as you go. Some of the campsites in the area are accessible only by water. Throughout the district are numerous picnic areas, river access points, trails, and historically significant buildings and sites. Call (573) 325–4233.

VAN BUREN

The headquarters for Ozark National Scenic Riverways, located off High-way 60, has a small visitor area where you can pick up maps and informa-tion about the riverways. Open Monday through Friday 9:00 A.M. to 4:30 P.M. Call (573) 323–4236. Visit the **Hidden Log Cabin,** John and Ash Streets, for a look at an 1872 home and the primitive furnishings used at that time. Small admission fee. Open Monday through Saturday 9:00 A.M.

to 5:00 P.M. April through October. The community celebrates **Current River Days** during the first weekend in October on Courthouse Square. It's an old-fashioned country fair with games, artists and craftspeople, country music, a street dance with square and round dancing, and contests. Call (800) OZARKVB.

DONIPHAN

The **Current River Heritage Museum,** 101 Washington Street, has displays on the heritage of the river valley since the early 1800s, including logging, military, and Civil War artifacts and information on early settlers in the area. Free admission. Call (417) 996–2212.

WEST PLAINS

This small town is the hub of a very rural area. The **Civic Center,** 110 St. Louis Street, presents stage shows with big-name entertainers, athletic events, and cultural productions. For a schedule call (417) 256–8087. The free **Harlin Museum,** 505 Worcester, has exhibits about people from the area and historical events. Open Tuesday through Saturday 12:00 to 4:00 P.M. Call (417) 256–7801. If your family wants some faster-paced action, check out the **West Plains Motor Speedway,** Highway 63, with races every Saturday night April through September. Call (417) 257–2112.

 Grand Gulf State Park, Highway W, with picnic sites, hiking trails and overlook areas, is almost on the southern state line. Often called the Little Grand Canyon, this park has a marvelous river gorge that was created when a huge cave collapsed. The river winds for a mile through vertical cliffs as high as 120 feet. Call (573) 548–2201.

MOUNTAIN VIEW

The **Wayside Park Trail,** East Highway 60, provides a short scenic walk past a log cabin, a railroad caboose, and three botanical gardens filled with native flowers. Free admission. Call (417) 934–2794. **Pioneer Days,** in mid-June, features musical performances, a parade, an arts-and-crafts show, a talent show, a classic car show, trick roping events, and more. Call (417) 934–2794.

FORT LEONARD WOOD

If you drive north you'll reach this army training installation, active since 1940 and responsible for training more than three million soldiers. At the free **U.S. Army Engineer Museum** on the base, you'll see exhibits on topographic engineering, land-mine warfare, tactical bridging, demolition and explosives, and arms and armaments. Open Monday through Saturday 10:00 A.M. to 4:00 P.M. Call (573) 596-4249.

LEBANON

Bennett Spring State Park, Highway 64, has a spring-fed stream stocked with rainbow trout, bringing fishing aficionados of every age to this 3,000-acre park. A hatchery in the park adds fish to the stream daily. Tours of the hatchery are available. Also in the park are hiking trails, a large spring, a nature center that is open year-round, campsites, a rustic dining lodge, and cabins. You can canoe on the Niangua River, which borders the park. Trout-fishing season is March through October. Call (800) 334-6946 or (417) 532-4338.

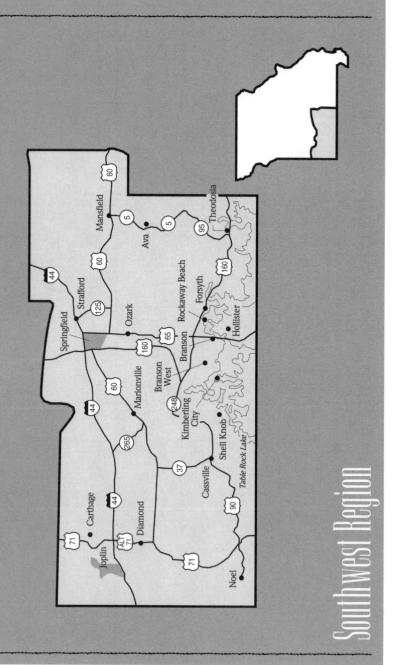

Southwest Region

Southwest Region

outhwestern Missouri offers countless opportunities for families looking for fun. Starting in the northern part of the region you'll find several small towns and the city of Springfield offering first-class attractions, including the birthplace of a nationally acclaimed children's author, a drive-through animal park, one of the finest caves in the nation, and a sporting-goods store that takes shopping to a whole new level of experience. As you travel southeast you'll find more than one million acres of federally protected wilderness land and two large lakes nestled in the Ozark Mountains. These ancient hills covering the southeastern part of this region are renowned for scenic drives when the wooded hills are dotted with blossoming wild dogwood trees in the spring or turned into kaleidoscopes of color in the fall. The city of Branson in this area has lured vacationers for decades and now is a music-show mecca with more than thirty-five theaters providing every type of family fare. To the west the region is rich in Civil War history, limestone caves, and lakes and streams offering water activities of all sorts.

MANSFIELD

Anyone who has read and admired the *Little House* books or enjoyed watching the television series will want to visit the **Laura Ingalls Wilder & Rose Wilder Lane Home and Museum,** on Highway A one mile east of the town square. The house where these wonderful classic children's books were written is preserved the way it was when the Wilder family lived there. Artifacts, family pictures, and possessions belonging to the Wilders provide you with a glimpse into the life of the woman who wrote the books that have been enjoyed by generations of children. A museum next to the Wilder home features exhibits of pioneering history as described in the books. Admission is $5.00 for adults, $3.00 for children ages six to eighteen. Open Monday through Saturday 9:00 A.M. to 4:00 P.M. and Sunday 12:30 to 4:30 P.M. Closed mid-November to mid-March. Call (417) 924–3626.

STRAFFORD

Travel west to this small town and you'll find more than 3,000 animals of sixty different species on display at **Exotic Animal Paradise,** a 400-acre game preserve 10 miles east of Springfield on Highway 44. Visitors drive along a 9-mile trail to get an exciting, up-close look at the animals, most of whom are roaming free. Don't forget to purchase a couple of bags of feed at the entrance, because if you feed them they will come—right up to your car window. The trickiest part—and the fun—is keeping their heads out of your car.

Halfway through your ride you reach Safari Center, where you can get out of the car, get something to eat, use the rest room, buy souvenirs, visit the petting zoo, and ride a pony or camel. You can go through the park at your own speed, but plan on spending two or three hours if you have young children. They won't be rushed through this place. Admission is $8.95 for adults, $3.95 for children ages three to eleven. Ages two and younger are free. Open daily 8:00 A.M. to 6:30 P.M. Open year-round, but off-season hours vary. Call (417) 859–2016.

SPRINGFIELD

The city of Springfield sits just north of the Ozark Mountains and is one of the fastest-growing areas in the state. Although for many vacationers this city is just a pit stop on the route to Branson, it deserves closer attention. There's plenty to do and see. Begin your exploration of this gateway to the Ozarks by picking up information at the tourist office located on Highway 65 at the Battlefield Road exit. Call (800) 678–8767 or (417) 881–5300.

Exploring a cave couldn't be easier or more enjoyable than the tour of **Fantastic Caverns,** the only ride-through cave in the United States,

The animals get up close and personal when you feed them from your car at Exotic Animal Paradise in Stafford. (Photo by Jane Cosby)

located just north of Springfield on Route 20 off Highway 13. A jeep tram carries you through this magnificent cave while the driver gives you a fifty-minute spiel that combines history, ecology, conservation, and geologic information in a way that even kids will enjoy. Admission is $13.00 for adults, $7.50 for children ages six to twelve; ages five and younger are free. Open daily 8:00 A.M. to 4:00 P.M. Open for evening hours March through October. Call (417) 833–2010. Wanna-be spelunkers can visit a smaller underground marvel called **Crystal Cave,** located on Highway H off Highway 44 north of town. This eighty-minute walking tour shows you beautiful cave formations and symbols that indicate Native American habitation in the cave. Admission is $5.00 for adults, $3.00 for children ages four to twelve. Open daily, weather permitting, 9:00 A.M. to 2:00 P.M. year-round. Call (417) 833–9599.

Most families don't have to be sold on the merits of a visit to the zoo, and the **Dickerson Park Zoo,** 3043 North Fort Avenue, provides all the fun and excitement that a good zoo should. It's designed to give kids an

Springfield's Fantastic Caverns is the only ride-through cave in the United States.
(Courtesy Fantastic Caverns)

exciting look at the animals, yet offers enough information to be educational and interest adults as well. Lovely walking trails lead visitors through carefully landscaped animal exhibits. There's a petting zoo where kids can purchase food and feed small animals. A "Missouri Habitats" area shows animals and habitats native to the Ozarks, including black bears, bobcats, and river otters. Admission is $3.50 for adults, $2.25 for children ages three to twelve; children ages two and younger are free. Open daily 10:00 A.M. to 6:00 P.M. April through September. The zoo closes at 4:30 P.M. October through March. Call (417) 859–2159.

There is a feeling of peace and tranquillity at the **Springfield Conservation Nature Center,** 4600 S. Chrisman Road, an eighty-acre natural oasis within the city limits. A visitor center provides interactive displays and activities for all ages. Even the youngest and wiggliest worm in your family will have fun, playing with puppets, assembling a tree puzzle, or examining items in the extensive collection of "found" natural objects on display. Six hiking trails range in length from a fifth of a mile to 2 miles, so all ages can be accommodated on a nature walk. An inside viewing area lets your family observe the mammals, birds, and other animals visiting the center's pond and feeders in any kind of weather. It's a great place to learn about and enjoy the natural beauty of the Ozark area. Free admission. Open Tuesday through Sunday 8:00 A.M. to 6:00 P.M. From April through October the trails are open until 8:00 P.M. Call (417) 888–4237.

The most popular tourist attraction in Missouri is **Bass Pro Shops Outdoor World,** 1935 S. Campbell Avenue. The minute you walk in the door you'll know why. In addition to the expected hunting and fishing supplies and equipment, this sporting goods store sells wildlife gifts, art, and jewelry; hiking and camping equipment; sports and outdoor clothing for men, women, and children; and boats and marine accessories.

There is a theme park atmosphere in the store, which includes a three-story waterfall; indoor rifle, pistol, and bow ranges; fish-feeding shows in a 140,000-gallon aquarium with divers and a video; a McDonald's Restaurant; a barbershop; a driving range and putting green; and a great seafood restaurant, Hemingway's Blue Water Cafe.

When you go, plan to stay at least half a day, designate a meeting place and time in case you get separated, and take a map from the person who greets you when you enter. You will need it. This isn't a store, it's an experience your family won't want to miss. Special holiday events are featured throughout the year. No admission. Open Monday through Saturday 7:00 A.M. to 10:00 P.M. and Sunday 9:00 A.M. to 6:00 P.M. Call (417) 887–1915.

Next door to the store is a **Fish and Wildlife Museum.** Here you can see mounted animals and fish that are displayed, when possible, in re-creations of their natural habitats. Although something of a monument to the sports of hunting and fishing, the museum provides a conservation and animal preservation message. Admission is $4.00 for adults, $2.00 for children ages five to twelve, or $10.00 for the entire family. Open Monday through Saturday 8:00 A.M. to 9:00 P.M. and Sunday 9:00 A.M. to 5:00 P.M. Call (417) 887–1915.

Cowboys shoppers shouldn't bypass **PFI Western Store,** Highway 65 and Battlefield Road. It's the largest Western store in the state and has more than 10,000 pairs of boots on display, an in-store radio station, a sixteen-foot video wall, and Western fashions for all ages. Call (417) 889–2668.

Children ages twelve and younger can unwind at the **Discovery Zone,** 319 E. Battlefield, an indoor playground of tunnels, foam mountains, and slides. For hours and prices call (417) 883–4FUN. **Hydra-Slide,** 4634 S. Campbell Avenue, offers a long, wet, slippery water slide for cool fun during summer months. For seasonal information and prices call (417) 887–8421. **Putt Putt Golf and Games** at 3240 S. Campbell has three eighteen-hole courses, batting cages, and a video arcade for a variety of family entertainment options. For hours and prices call (417) 889–PUTT.

Anyone with an interest in sports, whether as a player or observer, will enjoy **Missouri Sports Hall of Fame,** 5051 Highland Springs Boulevard. Interactive displays and authentic sports memorabilia document Missouri's greatest sports heroes in a way that kids will love. They can peer through the open window of a real race car, listen to five recorded pep talks by former St. Louis Cardinals and Kansas City Royals manager Whitey Herzog, hear themselves call play-by-play with the best in the broadcasting business, or experience taking a fast one over the plate from several of the greatest contemporary pitchers in baseball. Admission is $5.00 for adults, $4.00 for seniors, $3.00 for children ages six to fifteen, or $14.00 for the entire family. Open Monday through Saturday 10:00 A.M. to 4:00 P.M. and Sunday 12:00 to 4:00 P.M. Call (417) 889–3100.

Spectator-sports buffs can check out the **Southwest Missouri State University** Bears. The campus is located at Grand and National Avenues and you can choose from football, basketball, baseball, and soccer events. Admission fees charged. For schedules and prices call (417) 836–7678.

Located among rolling fields 10 miles outside Springfield at Highways 182 and ZZ is **Wilson's Creek National Battlefield,** a national park on the site of a bitter struggle for control of Missouri that marked the state's entrance into the Civil War. The visitor center offers engaging displays that children will find fascinating and a video that provides a good background on the people and events of the battle.

Self-guided auto and walking tours of the park let your family set their own pace as they explore the now-peaceful and serene site of this hallowed ground where more than 2,500 men died in one day. You can follow the course of the battle as you read the maps and historical information along the tour trail. Guided tours, historic weapons firing demonstrations, and living-history events are available in spring, summer, and fall. Admission is $2.00 per person ages sixteen to sixty-one or $4.00 per car. Open daily 8:00 A.M. to 5:00 P.M. Call (417) 732–2662.

Don't let the name **Snow Bluff Ski and Fun Area** confuse you. Year-round activities are available at this family activity center located on Highway 13 just 12 miles north of the city. Since the weather can't be depended on, artificial snow is created during winter months so that skiers can experience that downhill thrill that's not available in many places across the state. Ski rental, lessons, snow tubing, and slopes for beginning, intermediate, and advanced skiers are available. Summertime fun is provided by an extensive assortment of go-carts, a driving range, bumper boats, miniature golf, batting cages, and a video arcade. For prices and hours call (417) 376–2201.

Dean and Iler Berry and Tree Farm, located at 3650 W. Battlefield, offers your family the chance to pick your own produce or cut your own Christmas tree. The farm grows gooseberries, blackberries, red raspberries, pumpkins, and trees. For seasonal information and times call (417) 882–8664.

At Christmastime, Springfield celebrates a **Festival of Lights** beginning in early November and running through the end of the year. There is a Christmas parade to kick off the festival, and you can get a map of the Festival of Lights Trail so you can drive by buildings ablaze with lights, decorated in Christmas finery and sporting Christmas displays and scenes. The fairgrounds are aglow with more than one million lights and 400 displays. A train decorated with lights and designated The Santa Express transports Santa around the Springfield area so he can visit with children of all ages. Find out about hours and prices by calling (800) 678–8767.

The **Ozark Empire Fair,** the second largest fair in Missouri, is held at the Ozark Empire Fairgrounds on Norton Avenue. It runs approximately ten days in late July and early August. Live entertainment, livestock competitions, exhibits, food, and a glittering midway featuring carnival attractions of all types bring families in from all over the state. Other events throughout the year include horse, dog, and car shows; agricultural fairs; and rodeos. For a fair schedule and prices or a schedule of other events held at the fairgrounds throughout the year, call (417) 833–2660.

OZARK

Just to the south is this tiny town, which is almost a suburb of Springfield. If you have a family of big eaters, look no farther than **Lambert's Cafe: Home of Throwed Rolls,** Highway 65 South, for a refueling stop. During your meal, fresh-baked rolls will be thrown your way and you will be offered "pass arounds," side dishes that change daily and are provided free of charge. Huge portions, reasonable prices, a menu with enough choices to satisfy the pickiest of eaters, and a roll of paper towels provided on every table in lieu of napkins make this a family restaurant that can't be beat. Open daily 10:30 A.M. to 9:30 P.M. Call (417) 581–ROLL.

You won't find **Doennig Swings,** 671 Jackson Spring Road, in tourist guidebooks. This homegrown attraction features several barns filled with hay or mattresses and swinging apparatus rigged up for anyone brave enough to swing away. Parents are required to sign releases for children seventeen and younger. Hayrides, bonfires, horseshoe pitching, and paintball games are also provided. This place is not for the faint of heart and is best suited for older children and teens. If you or your kids want to swing on the wild side, this is the place. Take Highway 65 South then head east on Highway EE. Head for the barn with SWINGS painted on the roof. Admission is $7.00 per person. Open Friday 7:00 to 10:00 P.M. and Saturday 7:00 P.M. to 1:00 A.M. Call (417) 443–6600.

Ozark hosts **Village Days** during the month of June to celebrate the city's founding more than 150 years ago. The festivities include live entertainment, canoe races, tug-of-war contests, reenactments of famous gunfights, a petting zoo, a street dance, and games for kids. From November to early January the Finley River Park is dressed up with lights and displays for a **Festival of Lights**. A Christmas festival, parade, and lighting ceremony are held to kick off the season. For hours and dates about either event, call (417) 581–6139.

AVA

As you leave the Springfield area and travel southwest, you'll notice a change to rural, sparsely populated countryside, much of it natural and unspoiled. Across the southern half of the state, 1.5 million acres have been protected as national forest land. The **Mark Twain National Forest** provides recreation, nature study, and incredible opportunities for families wanting to get away from it all and enjoy natural splendor. Get information and directions before you visit, because you could easily get lost in these wilderness and semi-wilderness areas.

The **Glade Top Trail** is a 17-mile gravel road designated a National Scenic Byway. It offers your family the chance to view spectacular vistas of mountains and glades and catch sight of wild turkeys, deer, roadrunners, lizards, and other wildlife in their habitats. This area is especially beautiful during spring wildflower season and when the leaves turn in the fall. At the intersection of Highways 5 and 14, take Highway 5 south to Highway A. Turn south and continue to Smallet. Turn south on Gravel Road A–409 and continue to Forest Road 147, where the trail begins. The trail follows Forest Roads 147 and 149.

Hercules Glade is a wilderness area that offers more than 12,000 acres of isolated and challenging trails. Get directions before you go and bring everything you will need. If your family owns motorized recreational vehicles, you can use them on the 110 miles of trail at **Chadwick Motorcycle Use Area**.

JANE'S TOP FAMILY ADVENTURES IN THE SOUTHWEST REGION

1. Exotic Animal Paradise, Strafford, (417) 859–2016
2. Bass Pro Shops Outdoor World, Springfield, (417) 887–1915
3. Lambert's Cafe, Ozark, (417) 581–ROLL
4. The Glade Top Trail, Ava, (417) 683–4428
5. VanBurch and Wellford, Branson, (800) 492–4196 or (417) 336–3986
6. Shepherd of the Hills Homestead and Outdoor Drama, Branson, (417) 334–4191
7. Silver Dollar City, Branson, (800) 952–6626

Several campgrounds, picnic facilities, and hiking trails are available in this area. There are no admission charges to the national forest areas. For information about the Ava district of the national forest, call (417) 683–4428.

Bucks and Spurs Ranch, located south of Ava off Highway A, is a 1,000-acre working cattle ranch open to city slickers and others who want to try their hand at the cowboy life. You and your kids can enjoy trail rides along Big Beaver Creek and in the surrounding countryside adjacent to the national forest; participate in hunting expeditions; and share in the chores necessary to keep the ranch running, like driving cattle or riding fence with the ranch hands. Ranch-style meals are served on the trail or in the Ranch House. An unforgettable vacation is waiting for you if you're looking for a tourist experience that hasn't been prettied up. For prices and seasonal information call (417) 683–2381.

THEODOSIA

In the southernmost part of the region, this tiny town sits on the shore of **Bull Shoals Lake,** known for great bass fishing and less developed than the two larger lakes farther west. This part of Bull Shoals is the most rugged and offers a more isolated, relaxed experience than the lake areas closer to Branson. The main activities here are fishing and enjoying the unspoiled scenery and abundant wildlife that live along the shoreline. Camping is a popular activity here and at **Theodosia Park,** located just off Highway 160 at the bridge over the lake. You can find several campsites that have rest rooms, drinking water, and a protected swimming area with a diving platform. A small fee is charged April through October. Several free camp-sites are available at **Spring Creek Park,** located at the end of Highway HH. These sites have rest rooms, a playground, and a boat launch area. **Theodosia Marina-Resort,** located off Highway 160 west of the bridge, is a full-service marina where you can rent fishing boats, ski boats, jet skis, and tubes. The resort has a motel and five housekeeping cottages as well as a swimming pool, tennis courts, and a playground. For rates and availability call (417) 273–4444.

FORSYTH

As you travel to the west you'll encounter many small towns nestled in the Ozark hills. Some are on the shores of one of the lakes in this area and offer great water recreation opportunities. The scenic river bluffs along Bull Shoals Lake are great for wildlife viewing. At **Kissee Mills Park,** located south of Forsyth on Highway 160, there's a walkway and viewing blind overlooking a pond where you can see beaver, mink, and muskrat. Migrating waterfowl and shorebirds are abundant in the spring and fall. At dusk or dawn you can see deer, wild turkey, red fox, and bobcat along the shoreline. **Shadow Rock Park and Campground** on Highway 160 in town is a municipal facility with trailer and tent sites, rest rooms, and showers. Boating, canoeing, and fishing are available on-site or close by. Call (417) 546–4763.

ROCKAWAY BEACH

Rockaway Beach is a tiny resort community on the banks of **Lake Taney-como**. This 22-mile lake has a dam at each end and has unusually cold water. It offers excellent fishing opportunities but because of the water temperature is not conducive to most water sports. The lake is renowned for trout fishing—more than 800,000 rainbow and German brown trout are taken from it every year.

Along Beach Boulevard downtown are marinas where you can rent paddle-boats, canoes, pontoons, fishing boats, and fishing equipment and also hire guides. You can walk along the lakeshore and enjoy Rockaway Beach City Park, where you'll find picnic tables, a children's playground, free boat access, and a public fishing dock. Call (800) 798–0178.

BRANSON

You can't tackle this entertainment boomtown without a good city road map and a clear idea of what your family wants to do. There are too many choices and too many exciting attractions to wander around town without a plan. So make your first stop at the visitor center west of Highway 65 on Highway 248. Here you can get lodging information, show times, prices and locations, and more tourist literature than you can carry. Ticket prices to the shows range from $12.00 to $35.00 for adults and $5.00 to $17.00 for children. Most theaters offer three shows daily: early afternoon, late afternoon, and evening. Some theaters also offer a morning show. Organized family vacationers can call in advance and hit town ready to go. Call (417) 334–4136 or (900) 884–BRANSON ($1.50 per minute).

Branson has become known as the live-entertainment capital of the world—the city has more theater seats than Broadway. More than five million visitors a year come for the family shows and entertainment. Every show in town is appropriate for children, there is no gambling in the area, and there are few nightclubs. The entertainers put on enthusiastic performances and always seem to be having as much fun, if not more, than the visitors.

Although you can take your children to any show in town, they will enjoy some more than others. The best show in Branson, for any age, is the comedy, juggling, and magic duo of **VanBurch and Wellford,** at the Shenandoah South Theater on Highway 248. Your family will be amazed as VanBurch makes animals, people, and huge objects disappear before their eyes, or saws two ladies in half and exchanges their feet. And you'll laugh uproariously at the antics of Wellford, a juggling, fire-swallowing Emmy award–winning comedian. Call (800) 492–4196 or (417) 336–3986.

The first show in town was the **Baldknobbers Jamboree,** now located on Highway 76. This must-see show has been offering hillbilly music and laughs since 1959 and is still packing people in. Call (417) 334–4528. Another Branson original is the **Presleys' Jubilee,** on Highway 76. This show features three generations of the Presley family singing old country favorites, new country sounds, and gospel harmonies. They dance and cut up in a musical and comedy stage show that the whole family will enjoy. Call (417) 334–4874. The **Lawrence Welk Show** on Highway 165, featuring the Lennon Sisters and their family members, is a variety show that can't be beat. If your family enjoys lavish stage shows with singing, dancing, and fancy costumes, not to mention the Lennon Sisters and their singing daughters, you'll want to catch this show. Call (800) 505–WELK.

Several shows in town offer free admission to children. The **50's Variety Theater** on Francis Street off Highway 76 has a nostalgic musical revue of rock 'n' roll. Call (417) 337–9829. The **$25,000 Game Show,** at Roy Clark Theater on Highway 76, is an authentic game show that offers the opportunity to win cash and prizes. Roy Clark's show at the same location, **Branson's Royalty,** is a musical revue of his hit television show "Hee Haw" and provides free admission to children. Call (417) 334–0076. Kids are also free at the **Braschler Music Show** on Gretna Road, a country, gospel, and comedy show for the whole family. Call (417) 334–4363.

The **Dixie Stampede** dinner theater on Highway 76 is an unusual dining experience. As you sit and eat a four-course meal without silverware—it's all finger food—the show takes place in an enormous arena in front of you. The ninety-minute show features thirty performing horses, relay and buckboard races, and plenty of silly audience participation. Kids will love arriving early to see the stars of the show—the horses—in their stalls surrounding the theater. The food is excellent and the show is loads of fun. Admission, including dinner, is $29.95 for adults, $14.95 for children. Closed the week before Christmas until the end of March. Afternoon and evening show times vary, so for a schedule call (800) 520–5544.

At the **Ozarks Discovery IMAX Theater** on Shepherd of the Hills Expressway, you can catch one of several IMAX films. Movies start every hour and are shown on a six-story-high movie screen with a 22,000-watt sound system. The movie *Ozarks: Legacy and Legend,* which tells about the history of the Ozark people, is always playing and shouldn't be missed if you find these hills a fascinating place and want to know more about them. The forty-eight-minute movie was created just for Branson tourists and can't be seen anywhere else. Admission is $8.00 for adults, $6.80 for seniors, $4.80 for children. Open daily 9:00 A.M. to 7:00 P.M. Open later from June to October. Call (417) 335–4832. The **Gettysburg Theater,** at Highway 248 and Shepherd of the Hills Expressway, presents a two-act musical dramatizing events of the Civil War and how those events affect a family in 1893. It features a live orchestra and impressive speakers that surround you with music and sound effects such as cannon fire, artillery blasts, and galloping horses. Call (417) 334–8400.

The **Grand Palace Theater** on Highway 76 is the biggest and best theater in town and is the place for top-name entertainers and shows with big-city sophistication. Kenny Rogers, Barbara Mandrell, Billy Ray Cyrus, and Ricky Van Shelton are some of the entertainers who perform at the palace. The Radio City Music Hall Rockettes come in from New York each year after Thanksgiving for a Christmas Spectacular that shouldn't be missed if you're in town at that time. If your family goes for live entertainment on a grand scale, the Palace is the place for you. For a schedule of shows, dates, and prices call (800) 5–PALACE.

The entire city of Branson and the surrounding towns celebrate **Ozark Mountain Christmas** during the months of November and December. Almost every theater has a special Christmas show, and the streets, the Ozark hills, and most buildings are strung with lights and decorated with Christmas cheer. Several neighboring towns offer lighting displays, and bridges over the lakes are decked with lights that reflect off the quiet water for an enchanted atmosphere throughout the whole area. For information about special holiday events, lighting displays, and shows call (417) 334–4136.

The tourist influx to Branson started with the publication in 1907 of Harold Bell Wright's novel *The Shepherd of the Hills.* When you come with your family, visit **Shepherd of the Hills Homestead,** a mini-theme park on the west end of Highway 76. It's one of the best values in Branson. During a fifty-five-minute tour you can see places where the author stayed while writing the book and ride up 225-foot Inspiration Tower to get a panoramic view of the Ozarks. The one-price admission lets you enjoy a short horseback trail ride through the hills, pony rides, a Clydesdale wagon ride, a music show, and a great playground for the kids. Several shops and restaurants are also on the premises.

Each night a spectacular drama based on the book is staged in an authentic outdoor setting, featuring powerful scenes of masked vigilantes on horseback and a burning cabin. It is definitely a must-see in Branson and a show you and your children will not soon forget. The Homestead hosts special events throughout the year and has a wonderful drive-through lighting display during the Christmas season, as well as an outdoor drama based on the birth of Jesus. Open daily 9:00 A.M. to 5:30 P.M. Shows nightly at 8:30 P.M. A combination ticket, which includes all attractions at the Homestead and the drama in the evening is $22 for adults and $11 for children ages four to twelve. Call (417) 334–4191.

Silver Dollar City is a forty-acre theme park dedicated to turn-of-the-century crafts, music, and memories. It's located on Highway 165 southwest of town. Designed to resemble an 1890s mining town, the park features ten amusement rides including Tom Sawyer's Landing, a fantastic children's play area with tunnels and climbing structures that could keep your kids busy for hours. Country music shows take place in nine different theaters of various sizes, and more than 100 resident craftspeople demonstrate their skills and sell their wares in shops throughout the park.

Every evening concludes with a two-hour extravaganza of country music at the outdoor amphitheater. Shows throughout the day range from silly to serious and provide something for everyone's taste. McHaffie's Pioneer Homestead is a living-history area inside the park where your family can tour authentic pioneer buildings and join in the activities of daily life during pioneer times.

A tour of **Marvel Cave** is included with admission to the park, and you'll want to see for yourself how this cave lives up to its name. It has a twenty-story "Cathedral Room" and is the deepest cave in the state, not to mention one of the largest caves in the country. As you descend all the stairs, don't worry about little ones climbing back up. Cable trains return you to the surface from the cave's deepest point.

Every September and October, the **National Festival of Craftsmen** is held at the park and features the largest gathering of craftspeople in the

United States. People from all over the country join in this harvest festival to provide country music, craft demonstrations, and autumn food. **Old Time Country Christmas** is held November through December. During this holiday festival more than one million lights decorate the park, and Christmas music and holiday food are provided in theaters and restaurants. The atmosphere is alive with the spirit of the season, and the park provides a fairy-tale Christmas experience with carolers wandering about, a nightly tree-lighting ceremony, and holiday music filling the air.

One-day admission is $24.99 for adults, $14.99 for ages four to eleven; children ages three and younger are free. The park is open daily 9:30 A.M. to 7:00 P.M. late May through late August. For off-season hours and prices call (800) 952–6626.

Mutton Hollow Entertainment Park and Craft Village on Highway 76 is designed to give you a slower-paced experience based on the traditions of times past. A section of the park simulates an old-time county fair and features a restored antique carousel and a vintage Ferris wheel. Scenic trail rides over the Ozark hills are available, and craft demonstrations and old-fashioned country music and vaudeville shows take place throughout the park. This theme park has a more relaxed atmosphere than most and is a good place for families with young children. Admission is $10.52 for adults, $4.18 for children. Open daily 9:00 A.M. to 5:00 P.M. Call (417) 334–4947.

Water activities and wet rides are provided in a tropical-oasis atmosphere at **White Water,** a twelve-acre water park on Highway 76. The twelve rides include the 207-foot triple-drop "Paradise Plunge," a 500,000-gallon wave pool, the lazy "Paradise River," and "Splash Island" with tunnels, slides, waterfalls, nozzles, and pools just for the little ones. Life jackets and certified lifeguards are on hand so you can relax and let your children run free. Admission is $15.95 for adults, $11.45 for children ages four to eleven, $5.95 for seniors ages fifty-five and older. Open daily 10:00 A.M. to 6:00 P.M. from the end of May through the beginning of September. Extended hours June through August. Call (417) 336–7100.

You can enjoy a quiet cruise on Table Rock Lake on the elaborate 650-passenger **Showboat *Branson Belle.*** Each cruise includes a meal and a production in the three-story opera hall highlighting the showboat era of entertainment. You have twenty minutes after the meal to explore the boat, which may not be enough time for your kids. Ask for a window seat or leave the meal early if you want to see the views of the lake. The boat docks near Table Rock Dam on Highway 165. Tickets range from $17.95 to $29.95 for adults, $11.35 to $17.95 for children ages four to eleven. Cruises depart four times a day April through December. Call (800) 227–8587.

The **Sammy Lane Pirate Cruise** is a seventy-minute narrated tour of the White River and Lake Taneycomo that is definitely aimed at kids. They love the action when the boat stops at the Boston Ridge Gold Mine and is attacked by a fierce pirate. You can catch the boat downtown at 280 North Lake Drive. The *Lake Queen,* which leaves from the same dock, offers more straightforward sightseeing cruises and breakfast or dinner cruises with live entertainment. For cruise times and prices for both boats, call (417) 334–3015.

You'll probably have to **ride the Ducks** before you leave town, because your children will see them everywhere and clamor for a ride. So start your stay this way. You'll get a seventy-minute tour of the area, including Table Rock Dam and Lake, while riding in a rebuilt World War II amphibious vehicle. When you splash into the lake, the driver lets visitors drive—including kids. You can catch a duck on Highway 76 just west of Green Mountain Drive. Open daily 9:00 A.M. to 5:00 P.M. March through November. Tours run every twenty minutes. Tickets are $12.00 for adults, $6.50 for children ages four to eleven. Call (417) 336–DUCK. **Ozark Mountain Ducks,** located on Highway 76, also provide narrated land-and-water sightseeing tours. Call (417) 336–2111.

Thunder Road, on Highway 76 at the intersection of Gretna Road, offers activities for children of every age. Two miniature golf courses, single and double go-carts, bumper cars, batting cages, a bungee trampoline ride, a gyro orbiter ride, and the largest video arcade in the Branson area provide enough entertainment to keep the family busy for hours. No admission charge, individual ride tickets sold. Open daily 9:00 A.M. to 12:00 midnight March through October. For off-season hours call (417) 334–5905.

Kids' activities abound in Branson. **Pirate's Cove Adventure Golf,** 2901 Green Mountain Drive, offers two eighteen-hole miniature courses

See the sights in Branson by land and by sea when you ride the "ducks," rebuilt amphibious vehicles from World War II. (Photo by Jane Cosby)

with a pirates' hideout theme. A video entertainment center and gift shop are also on site. Open daily 9:00 A.M. to 11:00 P.M. Call (417) 336–6606.

Ridgerunner, on Highway 76, boasts the fastest go-carts in town and a slick track with greased corners, as well as a dirt track. There are five **Track Family Fun Center** locations on Highway 76. Each one offers a slightly different assortment of go-carts, miniature golf, bumper boats, and activity centers with rides for small children. Track IV is the biggest and, in addition to all the other activities, offers a course exclusively for licensed drivers. Track V features a McDonald's restaurant for families wanting a familiar meal.

Everyone complains about the traffic in Branson, but your family can beat it by renting a replica of a Model A at **Roadsters U-Drive** on Highway 76 and setting out for a scenic drive on the backcountry roads. Most of the cars are equipped with automatic transmissions and seat four people, if you count the rumble seat. Call (417) 335–2337. Another way to escape traffic is provided by **Table Rock Helicopter Tours,** on Highway 76. You can see the Ozark Mountains and the Branson area from on high and enjoy the breathtaking scenery below. Tickets start at $14.95 per person. Tours available 9:00 A.M. to 9:00 P.M. during the summer, 10:00 A.M. to 7:00 P.M. during the spring and fall. Call (417) 334–6102.

The **Branson Scenic Railway,** 206 E. Main Street in downtown Branson, offers forty-minute round-trip train rides that provide a relaxing view of Ozark Mountain valleys and ridges, many of which are inaccessible by road. You depart from the restored Branson railroad depot, which dates from the early 1900s, and travel in vintage luxury passenger cars complete with domed roofs. Tickets are $18.50 for adults, $13.50 for children ages thirteen to eighteen, $8.75 for ages four to twelve. Train departs three to four times a day. Box office open daily 7:30 A.M. to 4:30 P.M. Call (417) 334–6110 or (800) 2TRAIN2.

For a free look at the scenery at one of the best wildlife- and nature-viewing areas in the state, take a walk in the woods at **Ruth and Paul Henning Conservation Area,** on West Highway 76 just past the city limits. There is a scenic lookout area where you can get a spectacular view of the countryside. Use the nature trails for leisurely walks over the rolling hills or for serious exercise. Walk along the Boulder Glade Trail and watch for broad-winged hawks on the overlook, or look for tarantulas, scorpions, and lizards in the open glades. Call (417) 895–6880.

Downtown Branson has a renovated lakefront with an embankment topped by wide sidewalks and green areas with park benches, public fishing docks, and picnic spots. In **North Beach Park** you can feed the flocks of birds that congregate there. You'll find Canada geese, mallard ducks, and other water birds ready and willing to accept any and all food offerings you bring. Several full-service marinas are available for boat rental or access to the lake. For the **Branson Trout Dock** call (417) 334–3703, or call **Main Street Marina** at (417) 334–2263.

As you drive through town, your kids will notice a building on Highway 76 that is falling apart—or at least appears to be. That is **Ripley's Believe It or Not Museum of Amazement,** a strange combination of children's museum, freak show, and depository of oddball collections. It requires considerable reading and can be discomforting for the squeamish, so it's not appropriate for small children. But it features many wild and interesting things, some educational and some just weird. Older kids and teens will enjoy it the most. Admission is $9.95 for adults, $6.95 for children ages four to twelve. Open daily 9:00 A.M. to 10:00 P.M. year-round. Call (417) 337–5460.

One of the busiest restaurants in town is the **Branson Cafe,** located downtown on Broadway. It's one of the oldest restaurants in town and offers good, old-fashioned home cooking. If the tourists are lining up there, you can walk over and try **The Shack,** 108 S. Commercial. You'll find more locals here, and the home cooking is excellent and reasonable. While you're downtown be sure to browse around in **Dick's Oldtime 5 & 10,** 103 West Main Street. This wonderful store features more than 50,000 items stocked floor-to-ceiling and overflowing in the aisles. Shopping here is like stepping into a 1930s dime store. This is one shopping trip your kids don't want to miss.

If you want to be in the thick of the action, you can stay at the **76 Mall Inn** on Highway 76. This mall complex can provide a one-stop vacation destination for families. In addition to the hotel, you'll find a theater offering five country-music shows daily, a mall with twenty shops, an indoor tropical-style miniature golf course, and the Aladdin Arcade featuring electronic games. Call (800) 828–9068.

The **Settle Inn** on Green Mountain Drive offers rooms with a difference that are great fun. Thirty whirlpool suites are available, with rooms decorated in exotic or fantasy themes ranging from Sherwood Forest to Golfer's Paradise to the Circus Big Top. Family suites and standard rooms are also available. Laundry facilities are on-site. A comedy murder-mystery dinner theater is located at the inn, and there are two murders every week. Call (800) 677–6906.

The **Edgewood Motel** is located on Highway 76 amid the shoulder-to-shoulder Branson sprawl, but it offers twenty-seven wooded acres of green space for families who need some breathing, running, and playing room where they stay. Call (800) 641–4106.

Thousands of campsites are available in the Branson area. The **City of Branson Campground** is located on Lake Taneycomo and has 350 full hookup sites. Fishing docks, boat ramps, playgrounds, and picnic shelters are all available in downtown Branson year-round. Call (417) 334–2915. The **Old Shepherd's Campground** is located next to The Shepherd of the Hills

Homestead on Highway 76. It offers full hookup sites and wooded wilderness sites. Other features include a pool, game room, playground, convenience store, laundry and Sunday church services. Call (800) 544–6765. Another choice for camping close to the action on Highway 76 is **Presleys' Campground,** next to Presleys' Jubilee. It offers full hookup sites, as well as a pool, a playground, laundry, and showers. Call (417) 334–3447.

Compton Ridge Campgrounds and Lodge, located on Highway 265, has 234 campsites on eighty-five wooded acres. In addition to tent camping and full RV hookups, lodge rooms with attached kitchens are available. The complex includes three swimming pools, an indoor heated pool, a game room, a playground, laundry, and groceries and supplies. For rates and information on accommodations call (800) 233–8648.

TABLE ROCK LAKE

This 53,000-acre lake immediately southwest of Branson offers endless opportunities for boating, swimming, and fishing. Known as an excellent lake for bass fishing, it also has catfish, walleye and bluegill in abundance. The exceptionally clear water makes it a favorite with scuba divers.

A visit to the **Shepherd of the Hills Fish Hatchery,** located at Table Rock Dam on Lake Taneycomo, will show you where the trout in the lake originate. There are exhibits describing the process used to raise trout for release in the lakes. Guided tours and an introductory film provide a good overview of the area and the facility. Several aquariums will give your kids a close-up look at native Ozark fish. Trails beginning at the hatchery will lead you through a variety of natural settings, from the shoreline of the lake to the high rocky bluffs overlooking the White River Valley. The trails provide a great location for wildlife sightings and bird-watching. During the winter you can observe birds of prey, shorebirds, and aquatic wildlife feeding throughout the area. No admission charge. Open daily 9:00 A.M. to 5:00 P.M. Call (417) 334–4865.

The **Dewey Short Visitors Center at Table Rock Dam** has six different shows about the area's history, wildlife, and folklore, each one running from twenty to thirty minutes. Take your kids on an educational tour of the powerhouse to see how the dam generates power. Exhibits and a nature trail provide opportunities to learn more about the wildlife and fauna of the area. No admission charge. Open daily 9:00 A.M. to 5:00 P.M. April 1 through October 31. Call (417) 334–4104.

Table Rock State Park, located 1 mile south of the dam on Highway 165, has RV and tent campsites and a day picnic area. Call (417) 334–4704. The **State Park Marina** rents a wide variety of water vehicles, including jet skis, pontoon boats, ski boats, canoes, paddle boats, sailboats, and bass boats. Here you can also learn to parasail, scuba dive, and pilot a sailboat. For rates and availability call (417) 334–3069.

HOLLISTER

The drive south from Branson on Highway 65 offers a scenic view as you pass through rock outcroppings where the highway was blasted through the hills. In this tiny town just south of Branson is the picturesque **College of the Ozarks,** or C of O as the students call it. This four-year liberal arts college requires all students to work on campus to defray the cost of tuition. There are approximately eighty work areas located on campus, ranging from a theater and a radio station to a dairy farm and a bakery. Most areas on campus are open to the public, including Edward's Mill, where you can purchase whole-wheat flour, cornbread mix, and grits; a weaving studio featuring handwoven items from pot holders to clothing; and greenhouses where houseplants and flowers are sold. You can eat at the **Friendship House,** where all food is prepared and served by students. A complete buffet is offered for breakfast, lunch, and dinner Monday through Saturday and for breakfast and lunch on Sunday during the spring, summer, and fall. During the winter daily specials are offered.

Visit the **Ralph Foster Museum** at the college to see a collection of 750,000 items pertaining to Ozark history and folklore. Some of the most popular items include the Beverly Hillbillies' car from the television show, an enormous collection of weapons and firearms, a miniature circus and life-size stuffed animals. There is a hands-on discovery room for children ages four to nine where kids can crawl through a cave, try on clothing, and examine a wide assortment of objects, such as stuffed animals, doctor's instruments, rocks, magnets, braille documents, and drawing tools. Admission is $4.50 for adults, $3.50 for seniors; children ages eighteen and younger are free. Open Monday through Saturday 9:00 A.M. to 4:30 P.M. March through late November. Call (417) 334–6411, ext. 3407.

One of the best resorts in the country is **Big Cedar Lodge,** located off Highway 86 on Devil's Pool Road. Nestled in a fairly remote area of the Ozark hills, it is a picturesque place with landscaped grounds and buildings designed in the grand style of wilderness hunting lodges of the past. The property was once a private vacation spot for two wealthy businessmen and has a rich history of stories as well as a resident ghost. Luxury accommodations are available in several lodge buildings or in private cottages and cabins. A full range of recreation options are offered, including horseback riding, carriage rides, hay rides, tennis, nature trails, a fitness center, golf, fishing, boat rental, and full marina services. Call (417) 335–2777.

If your family can't get enough of water activities, you might want to consider living on the lake during your vacation. **Table Rock Lake Houseboat Vacation Rental** rents 65-foot houseboats that sleep up to ten people and come with fully equipped kitchens, shower and bath, linens, gas grills, and even a television, VCR, and stereo so your children can't accuse you of making them "rough it." There are miles of shoreline to explore on the lake and the water is usually calm, which means you don't have to be an expert to drive the houseboats. Instructions are provided before you're set loose. Rates range from $110 to $350 a day depending on the season. Located at the Long Creek Marina off Highway 86. Call (800) 622–3242.

The roads throughout this area provide beautiful panoramic views, but take them at a leisurely pace. You run the risk of you or your children getting extremely carsick. The rolling, dipping, twisting, turning roads are spectacular but can challenge even strong stomachs. For panoramic views of the lake take Highway 86 west from Highway 65, then go north on Highway 13. Much of this highway follows the Old Wilderness Road used by Indians, early traders, and settlers.

KIMBERLING CITY

This lakeside town sits west of Branson on the shore of Table Rock Lake and offers plenty of opportunities for water activities. Houseboats are available in this area from **Tri-Lakes Houseboat Rentals and Sales Inc.** Call (800) 982–BOAT. You can enjoy the lake in peace and quiet with a ninety-minute excursion on board a forty-nine-passenger catamaran, the *Spirit of America*. It is docked at Rock Lane Resort on Highway 165 and cruises from April through October. For hours and prices call (800) 867–2459.

During November and December, you can drive through a 1.5-mile light extravaganza, **The Port of Lights**. Located off Highway 13 on a peninsula that juts into the lake, the display includes animated figures, holiday characters, and a 120-foot tunnel of snowflakes. Free admission for family vehicles. Open daily dusk to midnight. Since the display is visible from the water you can Ride the Ducks and get a land tour and then splash down to the lake to see it from the water. Call (417) 739–2564.

BRANSON WEST (LAKEVIEW)

The little town of Lakeview was renamed Branson West to take advantage of the publicity being lavished on the live-entertainment mecca just to the east. Branson West is close to many lakeside resorts, marinas, and campgrounds located directly on Lake Table Rock. The **Tribesman Resort,** off Highway 76, offers family lodge units with full kitchens and a complete activity program. A full range of activities for children during the summer months includes picnics, ice cream socials, crafts, nature walks, and storytelling. There is a children's fishing hole and professional fishing guides can be hired. Call (800) 447–3327.

Talking Rocks Cavern, one of the most beautiful caves in the state, is located just south of town on Highway 13. A forty-five-minute tour of the cave is dramatized by animated lighting techniques and sound effects. Above the ground, a 400-acre nature preserve with hiking trails allows you to enjoy one of the most beautiful parts of the lake. Open Monday through Saturday 9:30 A.M. to 5:00 P.M. and Sunday 12:30 to 5:00 P.M. April through September. Call (800) 600–2283.

SHELL KNOB

As you leave the Branson area and travel west there are fewer attractions and vacation spots and more open spaces. The **Timbers Resort** is located off Highway 39 on a secluded, wooded setting in the Mark Twain National Forest at the foot of Shell Knob Mountain. It's on the main channel of Table Rock Lake and has completely furnished lake-front cabins complete with fireplaces. It's a year-round facility with a heated pool, a game pavilion, a playground, and hiking trails that cover 100 acres. For prices and availability call (800) 753–3082.

CASSVILLE

Roaring River State Park is located south of town on Highway 112 on the southwestern edge of the Ozark Mountains and features more than 3,000 acres of rugged, scenic terrain. There are caves, springs, glades, and forested areas in the park, most of which is preserved in a natural state. You can see where more than twenty million gallons of water per day gushes from a spring to form the headwaters of Roaring River. The stream is stocked daily from March through October and provides excellent fishing for rainbow trout. The park has a swimming pool, hiking trails, 200 campsites, cabins, a motel, and a stable where horses can be rented. Call (417) 847–2539. For cabin reservations call (417) 847–2330.

The **Cassville District** of the Mark Twain National Forest has camping and picnic areas directly on Table Rock Lake. The **Big Bay** area offers thirty-eight campsites, drinking water, rest rooms, and trailer space. Take Highway 76 south to Highway 39 south, then east on Highway YY. The **Piney Creek Wilderness,** more than 8,000 acres of hickory forest with steep ridge and deep hollows, has five isolated hiking and horseback riding trails that total $13\frac{1}{3}$ miles. To reach the trailhead, take Highway 76 east to Lake Road 76-6. For information call (417) 847–2144.

Crystal Caverns, not to be confused with Crystal Cave in Springfield, is located a half-mile north of town on Business 37. It is one of the state's largest living caverns and offers a large variety of cave formations for viewing. Open daily 9:00 A.M. to 7:00 P.M., March through October. Small admission fee. Call (417) 847–4238.

NOEL

Traveling to the southwestern corner of the state yields this tiny town flanked by three excellent canoeing streams, **Elk River, Indian Creek,** and **Big Sugar Creek.** You can arrange a float trip by canoe, boat, or tube on any one of these beautiful small streams, which are all rated for safe, family floats. **River Ranch Campgrounds** on Highway 59 has campgrounds, cabins, and RV sites. In addition, they will launch you 5 to 12 miles upstream and you can float back to your car or campsite. Floating season is March through October, weather permitting. For availability and prices call (800) 951–6121. Camping and float equipment rental is also available at **Dube's Three River Campground, Inc.,** at (417) 223–4746 or **Sycamore Landing,** at (417) 475–6460.

There are two caves in the area that are open to tourists. **Bluff Dwellers' Cave,** a living cave that once sheltered an indigenous civilization, also has a small museum of rocks, minerals, fossils, and arrowheads. Small admission charge. Open year-round. For hours and prices call (417) 475–3666. **Ozark Wonder Cave,** 4 miles north of town on Route 2, has seven rooms of natural formations. The tour includes Civil War stories and legends of buried treasure. Small admission charge. Open year-round. For hours and prices call (417) 475–3579.

DIAMOND

Head north to find this tiny town and the **George Washington Carver National Monument**. It's located west of town off County Road V, then south on County Road 16Q. The national park covers 240 acres of land that belonged to Moses and Susan Carver, the family who owned George's mother at the time of his birth and who raised him after the Civil War. Stop at the visitor center to hear the inspirational story of the slave child who grew up to become one of the greatest scientists of his day. Then you can walk along the short trails through beautiful wooded and prairie areas to see the Carver family cemetery, the 1881 Carver home, and the site of George's birth. It's also an excellent place for bird-watching and wildlife sightings. Prairie Day is held every September at the park and features activities that celebrate early pioneer life, including plant identification walks, living-history demonstrations, musical performances, wagon rides, and hayrides. Only picnicking is permitted in the park. No admission charge, donations requested. Open daily 9:00 A.M. to 5:00 P.M. Call (417) 325–4151.

JOPLIN

The city of Joplin is the hub of the four-state region where Missouri borders Kansas, Oklahoma, and Arkansas. The **Dorothea B. Hoover Museum,** located in Schifferdecker Park just north of West 7th Street, offers an in-depth look at family life in the Victorian era, 1840 to 1910. You can see a typical kitchen, dining room, office, parlor, and bedroom, and a miniature room equipped with the kinds of toys children of this era used. The museum also features more than sixty antique dolls dating from 1890 and an ani-mated miniature circus. No admission charge. Open Tuesday through Sat-urday 10:00 A.M. to 4:00 P.M. and Sunday 1:00 P.M. to 4:00 P.M. April through September. Closed until 12:00 and every Tuesday from October through March. Call (417) 623–1180.

A section of the old St. Louis and San Francisco Railroad roadbed has been cleared and smoothed into a hard-packed surface for biking, hiking, and walking. The 4-mile **Frisco Greenway Trail** runs between Joplin and Webb City and is accessible for wheelchairs and baby strollers. The trail is lined with trees, bushes and wildflowers. Call (417) 781–1664. You can rent mountain bikes at **Joplin Bike and Fitness,** 2629 South Main Street, which also sponsors training rides and races. Call (417) 624–2453.

Stock-car racing fans should check out the **66 Speedway,** 3406 West 7th Street. Races take place every Saturday night from March 1 through October 31. For specific events and ticket prices call (417) 782–0660.

Ozark Sunrise Expeditions, south of town on Shoal Creek, offers swimming, fishing, canoeing, and camping in a quiet, serene ten-acre set-ting. A picnic ground with volleyball, badminton, and horseshoe areas is also available. You can float on the creek in a canoe or an eight-person raft. You can sign up for a guided trip in the moonlight or in the middle of win-ter, and you can even go on a special "Horror of Shoal Creek" Halloween float trip. Classes are offered in canoeing, rappelling, wilderness camping, and outdoor survival skills. Take Highway 86 south, and turn left on NN Highway. Hot showers and RV hookups are available. Open year-round. Call (417) 782–5272.

You can see the beautiful bluffs of Shoal Creek from the back of a horse on trail rides offered by **Happy Trails,** located 2 blocks north of Highway 44 on Schifferdecker Road. This outfit runs guided trail rides for riders at any level of experience, horse-drawn buggy rides, and horse-drawn sleigh rides when the weather cooperates with a good snow. For prices and hours call (417) 781–7703.

JANE'S TOP ANNUAL EVENTS IN THE SOUTHWEST REGION

Bass Pro Shops Outdoor World Spring Fishing Classic, February
  to March, Springfield, (417) 887–1915
Village Days, June, Ozark, (417) 581–6139
Ozark Empire Fair, late July to early August, Springfield,
  (417) 833–2660
Prairie Day, early September, Diamond, (417) 325–4151
Silver Dollar City National Festival of Craftsmen, September to
  October, Branson, (800) 952–6626
Maple Leaf Festival, late October, Carthage, (417) 358–2373
Precious Moments Lighting Ceremony, early November,
  Carthage, (800) 543–7975
Festival of Lights, early November through December,
  Springfield, (800) 678–8767
Ozark Mountain Christmas, early November through
  December, Branson, (417) 334–4136

You can find some interesting things on backcountry roads, and south
of town you'll find a mini-petting zoo that's open to anyone with an interest
in animals. Not a true tourist attraction, **Keplar's Funny Farm** is a private
collection of exotic animals whose owner invites people to come and enjoy
his hobby. The animal population varies and you may see llamas, ostriches,
turkeys, deer, ponies, goats, geese, and a monkey or two. To reach the farm
take Highway 71 south 3½ miles, and turn right on Spurgeon Road. After
going exactly 3 miles turn left on Gum Road. The farm is ¼ mile ahead on
the left; you'll see the name on the mailbox. Watch your odometer—there
aren't any street signs marking these country roads. No admission charge.
Visit anytime from sunup to sundown. Bring your own bread or animal
feed. Call (417) 623–3605.

If your family has an interest in the strange and unusual, and isn't afraid of the dark, you can go looking for the **Spooklight**. According to local legend, an eerie light appears in the middle of a lonely road almost every night. It is often described as a giant ball of light bouncing over the hills and across the fields. It has been rumored to come right up to cars and land on the hood, then bounce off or disappear and reappear behind the car. As the legend has it, the light has been spooking people since 1886. To go looking for the light, take Highway 44 west from town to Highway 43. Turn south on Highway 43 and drive approximately 6 miles. When you see Highway BB is on your left, turn right on Iris Road. Drive approximately 3 miles to the end of the road and turn right. Drive 1 mile to the second dirt road on the left. Turn left here and drive ¼ mile. You are now on Spook Light Road. Park anywhere along the side of the road and wait. There are several roads off this one that you can turn onto and possibly see the "Light." Find a dark spot to wait—the darker the better.

At one time mining was a major industry in this area of the state. One of the largest open-pit mines in the world is now flooded, making it an ideal place for swimming and scuba diving. **Captain John's Sports and Scuba,** located north of town on Highway MM, has Blue Water Lake, a fourteen-acre flooded mine where you can swim or dive without being bothered by people fishing or boating. There is also a safe swimming area, as well as camping areas with RV hookups. Snow skiing is also available, with artificial snow. Or, you can learn rappelling skills on a 36-foot tower. For prices and availability call (417) 673–2724.

CARTHAGE

Immediately to the east of Joplin, Carthage offers an unusual variety of attractions for such a small place. The one that draws the most people is **Precious Moments Chapel and Visitors Center**. Take Alternate Highway 71 south of town, then go west on Highway HH and follow the signs. You'll find a visitor center, several gardens, and a Christian chapel that can all best be described in one word: cute. The site was built by "Precious Moments" artist Sam Butcher, and everything is decorated with murals and statues of the doe-eyed children that made him rich and famous.

The chapel has fifty biblical murals, exquisite stained-glass windows, wood and bronze carvings, and intricate wrought-iron gates. The gardens are beautifully landscaped and feature several unique settings. The Chapelaires, a gospel and bluegrass music group, perform several times daily. And several gift shops offer "Precious Moments" items of every size, shape, and material. Don't take any family member who can't tolerate an overdose of sweetness, but those who like that sort of thing are in for a precious and spiritual time. No admission charge. Open daily 9:00 A.M. to 7:00 P.M. April through October. For off-season hours and show times call (800) 543–7975.

This city was the site of a major battle during the Civil War and by 1864 was completely destroyed by guerrilla warfare in the area. The small **Civil War Museum,** 205 East Grant Street, provides artifacts and detailed information about the battle that was waged in this small town and the guerrilla activity from both sides that forced most townspeople to flee their homes. It's a great small museum that gives a powerful picture of a terrible time. Kids enjoy the battle diorama outlining the sequence of the fighting with miniature figures. No admission charge. Open Monday through Saturday 8:30 A.M. to 5:00 P.M. and Sunday 1:00 to 5:00 P.M. Call (417) 358–6643.

The **Old Cabin Shop,** located on Mound Street Road just west of town, is a strange combination of museum and business. On the property and open to visitors is an old log cabin built in the 1830s and used as the county courthouse in 1841. A newer building sells guns, muzzle-loading equipment, archery equipment, Boy Scout items, and beekeeping supplies. In the back of the store is a marvelously quaint small "museum" of the owner's private collections of Indian artifacts, toys, and old guns. It's a great rough-and-ready place and well worth a visit if you or your children are interested in these subjects. No admission charge. For hours call (800) 799–6720.

Every family has at least one collector, and you take yours to visit **Red Oak II** at your own risk. This conglomeration of assorted old buildings and works of art made from throwaways, located outside Carthage on Route 1, is the eccentric collection of artist Lowell Davis. After viewing the restored buildings, the outlandish outdoor sculptures, and the old pipes turned into a fountain, you will never be able to tell your kids not to drag junk home again.

Don't expect a museum-quality experience here. This place is just for fun and is not to be missed. Tour an old general store, a blacksmith shop, outlaw Belle Starr's home, a one-room schoolhouse, and a re-created cemetery. Stay at the Dalton Gang house or several other homes available for bed and breakfast. Give your kids the run of the town, but tell them not to chase the chickens that are roaming everywhere. Davis gained national renown for his porcelain figurines of barnyard animals, and the chickens rule the roost here. No admission charge. Open 10:00 A.M. to 6:00 P.M. Monday through Saturday and 12:00 to 5:00 P.M. March through November. Call (417) 358–9018.

The **Royalty Arena** is an indoor/outdoor 2,000-seat arena where you can see bull riding, horse and mule shows, concerts, and rodeos. For show schedules and prices call (417) 548–7722. Carthage lights up for Christmas in November and December with lighting displays in the downtown area, at the Precious Moments Chapel and Visitor Center, and at Red Oak II, and with the Way of Salvation Lighting Ceremony at the **Immaculate Heart of Mary Shrine,** located southeast of town. The shrine was built and is maintained by Catholic Vietnamese immigrants to the area and puts on a drive-through lighting exhibit from Thanksgiving through January 1. It features biblical scenes illuminated with more than 700,000 lights. No admission charge, but donations requested. For hours call (417) 358–8580.

Maple Lane Farm, a historic twenty-room mansion located east of town on Highway 96, is available if you'd enjoy staying in an architectural treasure located in a relaxed country setting. The bed and breakfast offers rooms decorated with family heirlooms, a farm with a barnyard full of animals for petting, a twenty-two-acre stocked lake for fishing, and acres of countryside for hunting or hiking. Rooms start at $50 per night. Day admission to the fishing, picnic, playground, and animal area is available for $1.00 per person. Call (417) 358–6312.

MARIONVILLE

You can reach this small town of 2,000 people, located on Highway 60, by traveling to the east. Marionville draws tourists from all over the world even though there is only one attraction—hundreds of albino, snow-white squirrels. It's one of only two places in the country where you can find these beautiful, scampering creatures; the other place is a small town in Illinois. Townspeople feed them, provide nesting boxes, and watch for predators that may threaten their special residents. Anyone wishing to see the squirrels in person, and not just imprinted on the souvenirs available everywhere in town, is advised to come on a cloudy fall day when the critters are busy collecting acorns and walnuts throughout the area.

Mid-Missouri Region

The middle region of the state is a land of man-made lakes. In the southern part of the region are two small lakes, Stockton Lake and Pomme de Terre Lake, both unspoiled and rugged. North of these are two large lakes: Truman Lake, surrounded by natural countryside and open spaces and, east of that, Lake of the Ozarks, with widespread development and tourist attractions of every type and description. But besides water sports and recreation, this region has the capital city; the Missouri Wine Country meandering alongside the Missouri River; the city of Columbia, home of the main campus of the state university system and the popular Missouri Tiger athletic teams; and Sedalia, the small city that hosts the state fair each year. So, there's plenty to do and see here.

NEVADA

This rural area has a lot to offer if you enjoy nature and wildlife. The **Schell-Osage Conservation Area** is one of the best places in the state for viewing wildlife. You can see waterfowl, pelicans, shorebirds, herons, turtles, wild turkeys, river otters, and—in the wintertime—bald eagles. In the fall, the goose population swells to several thousand and peregrine falcons follow the annual duck migration. To reach the area take Highway 54, then head north on County Road AA and turn east on County Road RA to the area headquarters. Call (417) 876–5226.

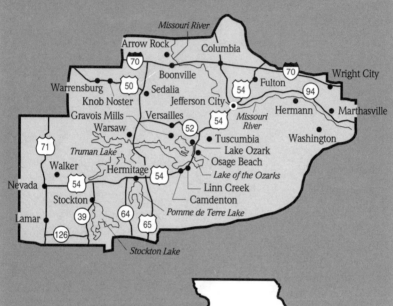

Missouri River

Arrow Rock

Columbia

70

70

Wright City

Boonville

Warrensburg

50

Sedalia

Fulton

Knob Noster

54

94

Jefferson City

Hermann

Marthasville

Gravois Mills

Versailles

54

Missouri River

Warsaw

52

Washington

71

Truman Lake

Tuscumbia

Lake Ozark

Walker

Hermitage

Osage Beach

54

Lake of the Ozarks

Nevada

54

Linn Creek

Stockton

Camdenton

Lamar

39

64

Pomme de Terre Lake

126

65

Stockton Lake

Mid-Missouri Region

WALKER

The **Osage Village State Historic Site,** Highway 54, preserves the location of what was once an Osage Indian village. There are no facilities at the park. But if you enjoy hiking, there is a self-guided tour of the area. Call (417) 682–2279.

LAMAR

At the **Harry S Truman Birthplace State Historic Site,** Highway 160, you can see the birthplace of the only Missourian to be elected president. Free guided tours of the home are available. Call (417) 682–2279. **Prairie State Park** features the state's largest remaining section of the vast tallgrass prairie that once covered hundreds of miles of the Midwest. There are bison, prairie chickens, elk, white-tailed deer, and coyotes in this 2,500-acre park. Take Highway 160 west, turn north on Highway 43, then go west on County Road K, west on County Road P, and south on NW 150th Lane. More than 10 miles of trails will take you past prairie streams, hundreds of species of wildflowers, and numerous wildlife habitats. Stop at the visitor center for trail maps and information. Nature programs are offered year-round. Call (800) 334–6946.

STOCKTON

Great sailing and fishing and miles of natural, undeveloped shoreline can be found to the east at **Stockton Lake.** If you and your family like the great outdoors, you'll enjoy the remoteness of this 25,000-acre lake. Twelve public-use areas around the lake offer boat ramps, picnic areas, fishing docks, beaches, campsites, and trails. Visit the information center at the dam on Highway 32 to get information about the area. **Stockton State Park,** Highway 215, covers more than 2,000 acres along the shore of the lake and has a motel, cabins, a restaurant, forty-five campsites, and a large marina where houseboats as well as fishing boats can be rented. Call (417) 276–4259, or (417) 276–5422 for motel reservations.

Stop by the **Missouri Dandy Pantry,** 414 North Street, to see the largest black walnut processor in the world. The gift shop has nuts of all kinds, candy, and hand-crafted items. Open Monday through Friday 8:00 A.M. to 5:00 P.M., Saturday 9:00 A.M. to 4:00 P.M. Thirty-minute tours of the processing plant are given Monday through Friday at 2:00 P.M. Call (800) 872–6879 or (417) 276–5121. The big event in this town is the **Walnut Festival** held the last weekend in September at the Stockton City Park. There are carnival rides, free nightly entertainment, arts and crafts for sale, craft demonstrations, a parade, and various competitions you or your children can enter. Call (417) 276–5213.

HERMITAGE

This small town to the northeast is right next to **Pomme de Terre Lake,** a small 7,800-acre lake where fishing and swimming are the main attractions. You can visit the **1872 Jail–Visitors Center** in the town square to find out about the area. It's primarily rural, but there are four marinas and several motels, resorts, and parks with campsites and picnic areas. In addition to enjoying lake sports, you can rent a canoe and float along the **Pomme de Terre River,** which shows few signs of civilization and promises a true get-away-from-it-all trip. For information about the area call (800) 235–9519.

Pomme de Terre State Park, Highway 64, has 700 acres along the lakeshore with campgrounds on either side of the lake as well as two public beaches, forty-six picnic sites, a hiking trail that leads to a platform overlooking the lake, and a marina for boat rental. Call (417) 852–4291.

WARSAW

Immediately to the north of Hermitage is Harry S Truman Reservoir, known as **Truman Lake.** Although it covers 56,000 acres, it is remarkably free of commercialization. Since the area isn't as built up as the Lake of the Ozarks to the east, boating is the primary diversion. The highways aren't lined with tourist attractions, but there are plenty of motels, resorts and campsites to accommodate those who want a natural, quiet vacation on the water.

Start your visit to the area at the **Harry S Truman Dam and Reservoir,** Highway 65. You shouldn't miss the visitor center's spectacular viewing room with two spotting scopes for visitors to observe the lake and wildlife. There is a reproduction of an archaeological dig of a Pleistocene spring located in the area, as well as other exhibits on local history. A theater provides films and slide presentations about the natural features of the region. Free admission. Open daily 9:00 A.M. to 5:00 P.M. March through

December. You can also tour the powerhouse exhibit area to view colorful displays explaining how the dam works to control flooding in the area. For visitor center or powerhouse call (816) 438–2216.

Surrounded by water on three sides, the **Harry S Truman State Park,** Highway 7, offers plenty of opportunities for water recreation. The 1,400-acre park has 201 campsites in the forest and on the lakeshore, and a boat ramp, a sand swimming beach, a full-service marina, and several hiking trails. Nature programs, presentations, and films are offered Friday and Saturday during the summer months. Call (800) 334–6946 or (816) 438–7711.

Go into the small town of Warsaw and walk across the old **Swinging Bridge,** Highway 7 and Main Street. This relic is one of many bridges that used to provide area residents with a way to cross the river. Or visit the **Benton County Museum,** 700 Benton Street, located in an old school and filled with unique historical items, many donated by local residents. Small admission fee. Open Tuesday through Sunday 1:00 to 5:00 P.M. Memorial Day through Labor Day. Open weekends in September and October. Call (816) 438–7462.

Fans of the Wild West will enjoy visiting **J&S Old Western Store and Museum,** 1038 East Main Street. In addition to the Western items for sale, the owners have devoted a section of the store to their extensive collection of saddles, blankets, bits, spurs, branding irons, and Native American relics. Free admission. Open daily 9:00 A.M. to 4:30 P.M. Call (816) 438–2631.

If your kids need a break from nature, take them to **Shawnee Bend Fun Center,** Highway 7. You'll find go-carts, a miniature golf course, batting cages, a video arcade, and a water slide. Open Tuesday through Saturday 11:00 A.M. to 8:00 P.M. Memorial Day through Labor Day. Call (816) 438–2546.

Every mid-July this area celebrates **Jubilee Days** downtown at Drake Harbor, with carnival rides, a street dance, kids' games, contests, a parade, and food and craft booths. A **Festival of Lights** is held from Thanksgiving through January on Friday, Saturday, and Sunday nights 5:30 to 10:00 P.M. Long Shoal Campground, Highway 7, is transformed into a free drive-through lighting display more than a mile long. Call (800) WARSAW–4 or (816) 438–5922.

VERSAILLES

This town (pronounced Ver-*sales*) celebrates the **Old Tyme Apple Festival** the first weekend of October. It features several categories of walks and runs, a fiddlers' contest, food booths, arts and crafts booths, and activities for the whole family. Call (573) 378–4401. The Royal Arts Council provides musical productions and performances, several for children, at the **Royal Theater** from May through September. Call (573) 378–6226.

GRAVOIS MILLS

The Lake of the Ozarks is a popular vacation destination with more than 1,000 miles of shoreline on a 58,000-acre man-made lake, one of the

JANE'S TOP FAMILY ADVENTURES IN THE MID-MISSOURI REGION

1. Truman Lake Visitor Center, Warsaw, (816) 438–2216
2. Ha Ha Tonka State Park, Camdenton, (573) 346–2986
3. Big Surf Water Park and Big Shot Family Action Park, Linn Creek, (573) 346–6111
4. Miner Mike's Adventure Zone, Osage Beach, (800) 317–2126 or (573) 348–2126
5. Hank Weinmeister House of Butterflies, Osage Beach, (573) 348–0088
6. Runge Conservation Nature Center, Jefferson City, (573) 526–5544
7. Katy Trail State Park, Missouri River Corridor, (800) 334–6946
8. Missouri Wine Country, Missouri River Corridor, (800) 932–8687
9. Arrow Rock State Historic Site, Arrow Rock, (816) 837–3330

largest in the country. The area offers hundreds of resorts of every type from world-class luxury accommodations, to small family-owned operations where guests stay in old-fashioned cabins and are treated like family. Powerboating is big at this lake, as are waterskiing, fishing, golfing, and tennis. This is the place to come to if your family likes plenty of activity.

The western side of the lake is less built up and in a more natural state than the crowded, highly developed eastern side of the lake. There are, however, many small resort communities on the western side where you can find a family resort to your liking. Many of the tourist attractions that bring people to the area are located on the busy eastern side. Numerous family resorts, motels, and condominums are available there. For information about resorts and attractions in the area call (800) FUN–LAKE.

The largest cave in the lake area is **Jacob's Cave,** Route TT off Highway 5. On a mile-long tour you'll see prehistoric bones, every type of cave formation, and evidence of three earthquakes. Admission is $10.00 for adults, $5.00 for children ages four to twelve; children ages three and younger are free. For hours call (573) 378–4374.

As you head south you come to the Niangua Bridge where you'll find **Forever Resorts** at Lake of the Ozarks Marina. You can rent a twenty-six-foot houseboat with five queen-size beds, a full kitchen, a television with VCR, central heat and air conditioning, and all utensils, towels, and bedding needed. Daily and hourly rentals and sightseeing cruises are also available. Call (573) 873–3705.

CAMDENTON

This town is the hub between the west and east shores of the lake. It's a small rural community that is home to many year-round lake residents, unlike some areas on the eastern side of the lake that have large numbers of summer-only residents. Every April this town celebrates the beautiful wild dogwoods blooming on the hills with the **Dogwood Music Festival,** held at various locations throughout town. Festivities include a parade, carnival rides, a petting zoo, a fine art exhibit and crafts show, bluegrass performances throughout the weekend, and Ozark food for your enjoyment. Call (800) 769–1004 or (573) 346–2227.

At **Ha Ha Tonka State Park,** Route 1, you can see both natural and man-made wonders. The remains of a magnificent castle built by a prominent Kansas City businessman and destroyed by fire are a popular attraction. But the 2,700-acre park, which overlooks the lake from towering limestone bluffs, also offers impressive natural scenery. The area is characterized by sinkholes, caves, underground streams, large springs and natural bridges. Scenic trails lead through deep ravines and bowls caused by collapsed caves, past a 100-foot natural bridge and a theaterlike pit called the Colosseum. There are picnic sites and trails for the handicapped. If you want to enter any of the caves, you must get a permit from the park superintendent at the park office. Call (573) 346–2986.

The romantic **Bridal Cave,** Route 2, has become a popular site for weddings thanks to a legend about an Indian wedding ceremony performed in the cave. Considered one of the most scenic caves in the country, it has several newly opened rooms that have doubled the size of the area open to the public. Guided tours are approximately one hour long. Admission is $9.50 for adults, $5.50 for children ages five to twelve; ages four and younger are free. Open daily 9:00 A.M. to 5:00 P.M. Extended hours during spring, summer, and fall months. Call (573) 346–2676.

LINN CREEK

This tiny town just to the north preserves memories of the past at **Camden County Museum,** V Road off Highway 54, in the old Linn Creek School. It features antique household furnishings, tools, and memorabilia from area schools, doctor's and dentist's offices, and churches. Open Tuesday through Saturday 10:00 A.M. to 4:00 P.M. May through October. Call (573) 346–4440.

The **Big Surf Water Park,** at Highway 54 and State Road Y, has twenty-two acres of landscaped water attractions, including a wave pool, a whirlpool spa, body flumes, a lazy river, and a "Bubble Beach" kiddie area specifically for children ages seven and younger. In addition to the water rides, you can play sand volleyball, Ping-Pong, shuffleboard, or horseshoes. Lifeguards are always on duty. Admission is $15.90 for adults, $12.90 for children ages three to eight. A significantly reduced nonswimmer's rate is available. Open daily 9:30 A.M. to 7:30 P.M. Memorial Day through Labor Day. Open weekends in the spring and fall.

Next door is **Big Shot Family Action Park,** with go-carts on a 1/4-mile track, bumper boats and wet racers, and an eighteen-hole miniature golf course. No admission charge, pay per ride. Open daily 10:00 A.M. to 5:00 P.M. March through October. Open until midnight during summer months. For either park call (573) 346–6111.

OSAGE BEACH

This area is the heart of summer activity at the lake and offers plenty of diversions for your family. Look for **Miner Mike's Adventure Zone,** east of the Grand Glaize Bridge on Highway 54. This indoor fun center features 25,000 square feet of mazes and climbing tunnels, a miniature-train roller coaster, Ferris wheel, and an arcade of electronic games, some of which are even educational. There's also an outdoor fifty-four-hole miniature golf

Big Shot Family Action Park in Linn Creek boasts the fastest go-carts at the Lake of the Ozarks.

course. A Cook's Tent sells kid food such as pizza and hamburgers. Tickets are $6.00 a person for either the maze structures or the rides. A combination ticket is $10.00 for both. Games take 25-cent tokens, with most requiring only one token to play. Open daily 10:00 A.M. to 10:00 P.M. mid-May through Labor Day. Call (800) 317–2126 or (573) 348–2126.

A big advantage to this play center is the huge outlet mall across the highway, which will appeal to parents looking for their own diversions. More than 100 top-name manufacturers' outlet stores at the **Factory Outlet Village** offer men's, women's and children's clothing and shoes, as well as housewares and consumer goods.

Pirate's Cove Adventure Golf, Highway 54 just east of Route KK, offers putting greens with caves, footbridges, and waterfalls. Call (573) 348–4599. Miniature golf is also available at **Putt'n Stuff Family Fun Center,** Highway 54 west of Grand Glaize Bridge. In addition to two golf courses, you'll find go-carts, bumper cars, and a special track for little ones. Open daily, weather permitting, mid-March through mid-October. Call (573) 348–2127.

A quiet, serene experience awaits you and your family at **Hank Weinmeister House of Butterflies,** Highway 54 approximately 1 mile west of Route KK. Inside the 3,600-square-foot enclosure you'll find twenty different varieties of butterflies flitting from flower to flower and even landing on guests. This garden of native and tropical plants is covered with black netting to keep butterflies in and birds out. A fifteen-minute guided tour provides information about the lives and needs of butterflies and what you can do to help preserve these beautiful insects.

As you walk through the enclosure, listening to symphonic music, you can observe the hundreds of butterflies kept here. Since they have an average life span of four to five weeks, approximately 100 new butterflies are added to the collection every week. If you or one of your children has a keen interest in these insects, don't leave without talking to the owner. His enthusiasm for his butterflies is contagious, and a visit to his attraction is a nice change from the hustle and bustle of other lake attractions.

If you visit between 9:30 and 11:30 A.M. you may see adult butterflies emerge from the chrysalises that hang on special racks. Admission is $6.00 for adults, $3.00 for children ages four to twelve; ages three and younger are free. A tearoom at the same location offers home cooking including homemade breads, pies, cakes, and other desserts. Open daily 10:00 A.M. to 6:00 P.M. April through mid-October. Call (573) 348–0088.

You'll find first-class accommodations at **Marriott's Tan-Tar-A Resort and Golf Club,** State Road KK, 2 miles west of Highway 54. In addition to luxury rooms and condominiums, the resort offers a complete range of recreational opportunities including bowling, fishing, golf, horseback riding, jogging, racquetball, parasailing, and tennis. The resort also has a health spa, a playground, a video game room, and supervised children's activities. You can rent boats of every type, motorbikes, mountain bikes, wave runners, and touring carts. The resort is open year-round. Call (800) 826–8272 or (573) 348–3131.

Good ole country music is available at the **Missouri Opry,** Route 2. It combines classic and contemporary country music, comedy, bluegrass, '50s rock 'n' roll, gospel, and patriotic music. Tickets are $10.00 for adults, $5.00 for children ages five to twelve; children four and younger are free. Performances are every night but Friday at 8:00 P.M. June through October, with special Christmas shows during November and December. Call (573) 348–2560.

Lee Mace's Ozark Opry on Highway 54 is the oldest country music show at the lake and offers traditional Ozark-style family entertainment. Tickets are $10.00 for adults, $5.00 for children ages twelve and younger. Performances are Monday through Saturday at 8:30 P.M. April through October. Sunday shows are offered on holiday weekends. Call (573) 348–2270. A little more glamour and glitz can be found at **Main Street Opry** on Highway 54. This show blends typical country fare with popular musical favorites. Tickets are $12.50 for adults, $5.00 for children ages twelve and younger. Performances are Tuesday through Sunday at 8:00 P.M. May through October. A special Christmas show is presented during November and December. Call (800) 843–9713 or (573) 348–4848.

If your family likes Mexican food, don't leave the lake without trying **Tres Hombres: A Mexican Cantina,** Highway 54. Look for the children's entrees on the menu, which has great fajitas, chimichangas, burritos, and taquitos for the big folks. Call (573) 348–6789.

You can rent houseboats at **SunSeeker Houseboat Vacations** located off Lake Road 54–37. Call (800) 798–9810. Or take a two-hour cruise of the lake at **Marina Bay Resort,** Lake Road 54-30A. Fireworks cruises are offered on Memorial Day, July Fourth and Labor Day weekends. Call (800) 377–6274.

Another first-class stop is the **Lodge of the Four Seasons,** State Road HH. It's a full-service resort with luxury rooms and condominiums along 72 miles of shoreline. The lodge has a complete fitness center and spa, golf and tennis facilities, seven restaurants, a full-service marina, a movie theater, and an extensive variety of sports activities from biking and cross-country skiing (weather permitting) to trapshooting and "walleyball." Call (573) 365–3000.

Lake of the Ozarks State Park, Highway 42, with 17,000 acres, is the largest in the state park system. There are 230 campsites available, half with hookups, and eight primitive log cabins are available year-round for those without an RV who don't want to pitch a tent. The park has two free sand swimming beaches, numerous picnic sites and shelters, boat-launching and -rental facilities, lake-view trails, and horseback riding. Naturalists present nature programs in an open-air amphitheater throughout the summer months. Nine hiking and horseback-riding trails cover more than 20 miles through the park. Guided hikes are also available. Call (573) 348–2694.

Ozark Caverns, off Highway A, is located in the park and can be explored with the help of handheld lanterns. The guided tour takes approximately one hour. You'll enjoy the visitor center with exhibits about the natural features of the cave and the area. Admission is $4.00 for adults, $3.00 for children ages thirteen to eighteen, $2.00 for ages six to twelve; ages five and younger are free. Open Saturday and Sunday 9:00 A.M. to 5:00 P.M. August 16 through the end of May. Open daily 9:00 A.M. to 6:00 P.M. June 1 through Aug. 15. During the summer months, specialty tours are available. For a tour schedule call (573) 346–2500.

LAKE OZARK

This area by Bagnell Dam is where everything started in 1931, when the Osage River was dammed to control flooding, provide electricity, and form what would become the most popular recreational lake in the state. The original 1930s strip area here is lined with all kinds of arcades, souvenir shops, and food shops designed to entice you to break your travel budget. A short free tour of the dam shows how electricity is generated and how the dam was built. Tours offered Wednesday through Sunday. Call (573) 365–9330.

An excursion boat at **Casino Pier,** immediately west of the dam, offers one- or two-hour sightseeing cruises from Memorial Day through Labor Day. Tickets are $8.00 or $10.00 for adults, $4.00 or $5.00 for children ages twelve and younger. Breakfast and dinner buffet cruises are also available. Cruises leave at 10:00 A.M., 12:00, 2:00, and 4:00 P.M. Labor Day through October, weather permitting. The dock has a cafe and a small trolley that brings you down the steep hill to the waterfront. Call (573) 365–2020.

The paddle wheeler *Tom Sawyer,* at the west end of the dam, offers narrated one-and two-hour cruises with a captain who was born and raised in the area. Your kids can feed giant fish from the dock. Tickets are $7.95 or $9.95 for adults, $4.00 for children ages twelve to six; ages five and younger are free. Cruises leave at 10:00 A.M., 12:00, 4:00, and 6:00 P.M. Memorial Day through Labor Day. If you would rather take to the skies, you can catch a helicopter here for a scenic ride over the Ozark hills. For prices and flight times, or for cruise information, call (573) 365–3300. Waverunners, jet skis, and boats can be rented at **Mike Fink's Marina,** 2 blocks south of the dam on Highway 54. Call (573) 365–6557.

If you're interested in seeing the river on the other side of the dam, float along the Osage River from the base of the dam past sleepy little river towns east of the lake area. The **Lazy "K" Campground** (Highway 54 north then east on Route V) rents canoes, and you can float on either a 5- or 12-mile stretch of the river. Call (573) 365–1374. Tour **Fantasy World Caverns,** Highway 54 north of the dam, and you'll see fantastic cave formations and a large underground lake. Admission fee charged. Open daily 9:30 A.M. to 5:30 P.M. May through September. Call (573) 392–2115.

The Osage Beach and Lake Ozark area lights up for the holidays during the **Lake Lights Festival** in November and December. Holiday activities include a parade and Christmas shows. Tan-Tar-A Resort is also lit up and offers free holiday activities. Call (800) 451–4117 or (573) 365–3002.

TUSCUMBIA

The **Miller County Historical Society Museum,** located on Highway 52 west, is a wonderful example of a free rural museum organized and oper-ated by dedicated volunteers who simply want to preserve their past. The museum's two floors of exhibits examine life in this region before the lake was created. Antique items highlighting Native American heritage and early pioneer home accessories, machines, and crafts are displayed in the old Anchor Mill building. Open Monday, Wednesday, and Friday 10:00 A.M. to 4:00 P.M. June through September.

JEFFERSON CITY

To the north and east of Tuscumbia is the state capital, with the **State Capitol** building, on High Street, sitting high atop a bluff overlooking the Missouri River. A museum on the first floor has exhibits about the state; guided tours are available daily on the hour from 8:00 to 11:00 A.M. and from 1:00 to 4:00 P.M. Visit when the legislature is in session from January through mid-May, and you can show your children how laws are enacted by watching from the visitor gallery Tuesday, Wednesday, or Thursday mornings. Call (573) 751–4127.

A number of historic buildings also are located downtown near the Capitol. The **Governor's Mansion,** directly across the street, is the home of the state's top executive. Tours are conducted Tuesday and Thursday 10:00 A.M. to 12:00 and 1:00 to 3:00 P.M. Call (573) 751–4141. The **Cole County Historical Museum** on Madison Street displays the inau-gural ballgowns of former first ladies of the state, as well as other state memorabilia. The top floor houses Grandma's Attic, with toys and artifacts of particular interest to children. Small admission fee. Open Tuesday 10:30 A.M. to 3:30 P.M., Wednesday through Saturday 12:00 to 3:30 P.M. Call (573) 635–1850.

The **Jefferson Landing State Historic Site** has three separate build-ings, two of which offer tours. Start at the Lohman Building visitor center, where you can take a short self-guided tour of the exhibits and see a fifteen-minute slide presentation on the history of the city. The Union Hotel next door has art and cultural exhibits and houses the Amtrak station on the first floor. Open 10:00 A.M. to 4:00 P.M. Call (573) 751–3475.

The State Capitol sits high atop a bluff overlooking the Missouri River and Jefferson City.
(Courtesy Missouri Division of Tourism)

Genealogy buffs and anyone who likes to dig around in old records can access all sorts of information stored by the State Archives and Records Division at the **Missouri State Information Center,** 620 West Main Street. Let your kids look up information about your ancestors. Who knows what you might uncover? County courthouse records; military records; land purchase records; birth, death, and marriage certificates; and more can be viewed on microfilm for free. Open Monday through Friday 8:00 A.M. to 5:00 P.M. Open Thursday until 9:00 P.M. Call (573) 751–3280.

At **Missouri Highway Patrol Safety Education Center,** 1510 East Elm Street, your kids can test their emergency reaction time, see the wreckage of a car crash in which passengers' lives were saved by seatbelts, look at illegal drugs and learn about the effects of drug abuse, see a 1931 Model A Ford Roadster like the ones driven by the first highway patrolmen, and view antique and homemade weapons and many other law enforcement items. Free admission. Open Monday through Friday 9:00 A.M. to 5:00 P.M. Call (573) 751–3313.

Runge Conservation Nature Center, 2901 West Truman Boulevard, is a beautiful interactive center, operated by the Missouri Conservation Department, that features hands-on exhibits about the wildlife and vegetation of this area. Your kids will love "Bubba," an enormous model of a bullfrog; the 2,500-gallon aquarium; the walk-through cave; and the wildlife viewing area. Free admission. Open daily 8:00 A.M. to 6:00 P.M. Five short nature trails surround the center, which offers a complete schedule of nature programs, guided hikes, and films year-round. Call (573) 526–5544.

Stop at **Central Dairy,** 610 Madison Street, for an ice-cream treat and choose from more than forty flavors. Owned by the same family since the 1920s, this dairy has been making and serving delicious ice cream for decades. Call (573) 635–6148.

As you head east, follow Highway 94 and the Missouri River for a winding, dipping ride and scenic views of the bluffs and the wildlife that live along the river corridor. You are now in the heart of the Missouri Wine Country and you will begin to notice vineyards alongside the roads.

This is approximately the same route followed by the **Katy Trail State Park,** the longest hiking and biking trail in the state. The trail cuts across the northern part of this region of the state. It starts in St. Charles in the eastern part of the state and follows the Missouri River all the way to Booneville, then turns south to Sedalia. Trail parking is available at many of the small towns that border it: Augusta, Dutzow, Marthasville, Teloar, Jefferson City, Columbia, Rocheport, and Booneville. The easy grade of this trail makes it perfect for family cycling or hiking. All sections of the trail may not be open; call for information before you set out. For trail information and maps call (800) 334–6946.

HERMANN

This proud community was inundated with German immigrants in the mid-1800s because it resembled their Rhine Valley homeland. The current residents maintain both the German heritage and the winemaking tradition with pride and enthusiasm. Start at the visitor center, 306 Market Street, where you can pick up information and maps of the area. Open daily 9:00 A.M. to 5:00 P.M. Call (800) 932–8687.

Learn all about this historic area at the **German School Building,** Fourth and Schiller Streets. On the upper floor of the schoolhouse is a museum with a mock-up of a pilot house, a bell from an old steamboat, models of boats, and a children's room with displays of toys, games, and dolls. Small admission fee for the museum. The first floor houses handmade crafts for sale. You can also pick up information about the town and maps for walking tours of historic buildings. Open daily 10:00 A.M. to 4:00 P.M. Call (573) 486–2017.

A twenty-minute tour of the **Stone Hill Winery,** Route 1, is fascinating even if you're not a wine drinker. This winery dates back to 1847, and the tour takes you through the enormous brick Main House and the vaulted catacomb wine cellars before ending with a free sample of wine or grape juice. The winery's hilltop grounds are steeped in history and charm and provide a perfect place for a picnic. Small admission fee for the tour. Tours and tasting Monday through Saturday 8:30 A.M. until dusk, Sunday 11:00 A.M. to 6:00 P.M. A gift shop sells wine, cheese, sausage, and souvenirs. Call (800) 909–WINE.

Hermann celebrates **Maifest** on the third weekend of May, with two parades, children's activities in the park, beer and wine gardens, German music and dancing, carnival rides, and activities throughout the town. During December there is a **Christmas Park of Dreams** with a walking trail of animated lighting displays in Hermann City Park. Admission fee charged. Open 6:00 to 10:00 P.M. Friday, Saturday, and Sunday from Thanksgiving to Christmas. Other holiday activities take place throughout the town. Call (800) 932–8687.

You can ride rails into town if you like. Amtrak has four stops daily; for a schedule call (800) USA–RAIL.

WASHINGTON

This tiny river town is home to the only manufacturer of corn-cob pipes in the world: **Missouri Meerschaum,** 400 West Front Street. An old display room allows you to peruse an extensive collection of pipes. Free admission. Open Monday through Friday 8:00 to 11:00 A.M. and 1:00 to 3:00 P.M. Call (314) 239–2109.

The biggest event is this small town is the **Washington Town and Country Fair,** held the first Wednesday of August at the Washington Fairgrounds, West Fifth. The Main Stage provides big-name entertainers each evening of the fair, and the Motor Sports Area has events like truck and tractor pulls, motocross racing, and mud races. Carnival rides, livestock shows, an air show, and food booths provide all the ingredients needed for a great time. This is the perfect fair for families on a budget since the one-price admission charge is good for all fair activities. Five-day admission is $20 for adults, $12 for children ages six to eleven; ages five and younger are free. Single-day admission is $8.00 to $12.00 for adults, $5.00 to $7.00 for children, depending on the day of the week. Call (314) 239–2715.

MARTHASVILLE

Dozens of authentic old German farm skills are demonstrated during **Deutsch Country Days,** held the third weekend in October at Luxenhaus Farm, Highway O. This extraordinary living-history event takes place on a farm that is home to eighteen salvaged historic buildings. This event is the only time during the year that the farm is open to the public. Crafts and skills demonstrated include wheat weaving, crosscut sawing, sheep shearing, natural dyeing, hickory-seat weaving, and many more. Many of the tour guides and demonstrators for the weekend are high school students in Future Farmers of America. Tickets are $8.00 for adults, $3.00 for children ages six to twelve; ages five and younger are free. Open 9:30 A.M. to 5:00 P.M. Saturday and Sunday during the event. Call (314) 433–5669.

WRIGHT CITY

Head up north to this small town on Highway 70 and eat at **Big Boy's Restaurant,** on the Highway Access Road. This family restaurant specializing in fried chicken and home cooking has been satisfying big appetites since 1924. Call (314) 745–2200.

FULTON

In this small college town to the west, you can show your children a piece of the Iron Curtain. A twelfth-century church, **St. Mary Aldermanbury Church,** was rebuilt here to serve as the **Winston Churchill Memorial and Library** at Westminster College, Westminster Avenue and Seventh Street. This is where Churchill coined the term "Iron Curtain" in a speech after World War II. After the fall of the Berlin Wall, a 30-foot graffiti-covered section of it was used as the basis for a massive sculpture that now stands in front of the church. Concerts, special activities, and services are held in the church. There is also a museum with exhibits about the life of the British statesman. Museum admission $2.50 for adults; children ages twelve and younger are free. Open daily 10:00 A.M. to 4:30 P.M. Call (573) 642–6648.

COLUMBIA

Sitting halfway between St. Louis and Kansas City, this city looks like a typical college town, but in fact it's a three-college town. The largest campus is part of the University of Missouri system, and two smaller, private colleges are also located here. Consequently, when school is in session there are college-age students everywhere.

Founded in 1839, the **University of Missouri** is the oldest land-grant university west of the Mississippi, and some of the older, hallowed halls of learning here seem steeped in tradition. Don't miss walking around historic Francis Quadrangle, the heart of the campus. You'll see six Ionic columns, all that remains of Academic Hall since a fire destroyed it in 1892. The eighteen surrounding buildings are on the National Register of Historic Places. Teens will enjoy touring the large campus and checking out the various colleges and programs. You can pick up information at the **Donald W. Reynolds Alumni and Visitor Center,** Conley Avenue, across from the Quadrangle. You may be able to join up with a scheduled group to get a free tour of the campus. Open daily 8:00 A.M. to 5:00 P.M. Call (573) 882–6333.

Several free on-campus museums are worth a visit. Check out the **Museum of Art and Archeology,** Pickard Hall. It's the third largest art collection in the state. Open Tuesday through Friday 9:00 A.M. to 5:00 P.M., Saturday and Sunday 12:00 to 5:00 P.M. Call (573) 882–3591. The **Museum of Anthropology,** housed in Swallow Hall, has items representing Native American cultures and state history. For hours call (573) 882–3764. If creepy-crawlies are to your liking, check out the **Entomology Museum** in the Agricultural Building. It has the largest university collection of preserved insects in the world. Call (573) 882–2410.

To really feel at home here, you must attend a **Mizzou Tigers** game. During home football games everything seems focused on Faurot Field,

Providence Road, and Stadium Boulevard. The team competes in the Big Twelve Conference, and residents all over the state, alumni or not, follow the games. Basketball is also big news, and you can watch the men's and women's teams at **Hearnes Center,** Stadium Boulevard and Mick Deaver Drive. Other MU teams include baseball, track and field, wrestling, and gymnastics. Pick up a complete semester schedule in Hearnes Center or call (800) 228–7297.

The university has a theater department that performs in several locations. A full schedule of dramas, comedies, musicals, and experimental shows are directed and performed by students September through April. Some productions may not be suitable for children, but you can call for a schedule and description. Tickets range from $5.00 to $10.00 Call (573) 882–PLAY.

Rock Bridge Memorial State Park, Highway 63, is just outside of town and has several interesting features to explore, including Devil's Icebox Cave, a natural rock bridge, and numerous sinkholes. A boardwalk and trails lead visitors to the geologic formations and through prairie and wooded areas. Call (573) 449–7402.

Don't expect sylvan vistas and beautiful hiking trails at **Finger Lakes State Park,** Highway 63. Although it doesn't look like anything to brag about, it may be one of your kids' favorite spots. This old strip-mining area is now used for swimming, fishing, and canoeing. The holes left from the strip mining have resulted in excellent swimming lakes, and one has a sand beach. But be warned that the swimming holes are extremely deep and there are no shallow areas. Make sure all children wear life jackets. This park permits the use of off-road motorcycles and all-terrain vehicles. Picnic areas and campgrounds are also available. Call (573) 443–5315.

The **Walters Boone County Historical Museum and Visitors Center,** 3801 Ponderosa Street, has numerous exhibits on westward expansion along the Booneslick Trace and on the heritage of Boone County. Free admission. Open Wednesday, Saturday and Sunday 1:00 to 4:00 P.M. November to March. Open 1:00 to 5:00 P.M. Tuesday to Sunday April through October. Call (573) 443–8936.

Your kids will love watching their own pizza being made at **Shakespeare's Pizza & Wine Bar,** 225 South Ninth Street. Go early in the

JANE'S TOP ANNUAL EVENTS IN THE MID-MISSOURI REGION

Dogwood Music Festival, April, Camdenton, (800) 769–1004
   or (573) 346–2227

Maifest, third weekend of May, Hermann, (800) 932–8687

Jubilee Days, mid-July, Warsaw, (800) WARSAW–4 or
   (816) 438–5922

Missouri State Fair, August, Sedalia, (800) 422–FAIR or
   (816) 530–5600

Washington Town and Country Fair, first Wednesday in August,
   Washington (314) 239–2715

Walnut Festival, last weekend in September, Stockton,
   (417) 276–5213

Heritage Days, mid-October, Arrow Rock, (816) 837–3210 or
   (816) 837–3443

Old Tyme Apple Festival, end of October, Versailles,
   (573) 378–4401

evening to avoid the crowd. Call (573) 449–2454. If you want to eat on campus, go to the Old Heidelberg Restaurant, 410 South Ninth Street. It has been feeding students for more than thirty years and serves breakfast, lunch, and dinner. Call (573) 449–6927. For a great family restaurant try **The 63 Diner,** Highway 63. You'll know you are there when you see the pink Cadillac jutting from the front of the building. They serve great diner-type food and the children's meals are served in cardboard cars. Call (573) 443–2331.

In July you can attend the **Boone County Fair and Horse Show,** held at the fairgounds, 5212 North Oakland Gravel Road. The fair always features a midway of carnival rides, live entertainment, horse shows, tractor pulls, and shows of various kinds. For admission prices and hours call (573) 474–9435.

BOONVILLE

This little town on the river has a proud history and approximately 400 homes on the National Register of Historic Places, making it a picturesque place to visit. **Thespian Hall,** Main and Vine Streets, is the oldest theater west of the Allegheny Mountains and hosts the annual Big Muddy Folk Festival, a traditional-arts festival held in early April. In August there is a special children's performance at the hall. The **Old Cooper County Jail and Hanging Barn,** 614 East Morgan Street, has an old jail and marshal's office you can tour. Small admission fee. Open Monday through Friday 9:00 A.M. to 5:00 P.M., Saturday 10:00 A.M. to 5:00 P.M., Sunday 1:00 to 4:00 P.M. from Memorial Day through Labor Day. For information about attractions in town call (816) 882–7977.

Boone's Lick State Historic Site, Highway 187, is a small park with a self-guided trail that leads down a hillside to the salt springs where Daniel Boone's sons once operated a salt-manufacturing business. No facilities in the park except picnic areas. Call (816) 837–3330.

ARROW ROCK

Settlers heading west in the last century founded this town that sits on a bluff of the Missouri River where Osage Indians once gathered flint to make arrowheads. During the twentieth century, progress bypassed this tiny town, but the residents have turned this to their advantage. They have done a remarkable job of preserving the past while inviting modern tourists to visit and enjoy a truly unique experience.

A free visitor center at the **Arrow Rock State Historic Site,** Highway 41, has exhibits and dioramas about the famous people who lived here and the events that took place in this area. For a small fee, you can sign up for a walking tour of the town. The 167-acre historic site has hiking trails and a campground with forty-three sites. Call (816) 837–3330. There are nine historic buildings in town open to the public, including the Old Stone Jail, the home of artist George Caleb Bingham, and the Old Tavern where you can eat in an 1800s atmosphere. Gun buffs and small boys will enjoy the extensive gun collection at the John P. Sites, Jr. Pioneer Gunshop.

Enjoy a wonderful family production at the state's oldest professional regional theater. The **Lyceum Theater** provides a full schedule of productions in a beautiful old Baptist church, Wednesday through Sunday from June through August. Reservations are recommended. For times and ticket prices call (816) 837–3311.

SEDALIA

As you head south you'll reach this prairie town that plays host to the ten-day **Missouri State Fair** each year in August. The fair is held on the State Fairgrounds, Highway 65, and always features a gigantic midway of carnival rides. This event includes agricultural exhibits and shows presenting the state's finest in crops and livestock; big-name entertainers performing nightly; displays and contests of traditional homemaking skills such as canning, baking, and quilting; rodeo performances; tractor and animal pulls; motorcycle stunt shows, auto races and demolition derbies; and other contests and shows of all kinds. It's the perfect place to take kids because there are always several petting zoos and other varieties of family entertainment throughout the fairgrounds.

Admission to the fairgrounds is $4.00 for adults; children ages twelve and younger are free. Parking is $2.00 per vehicle. Performances, events, and activities are individually priced. Special prices and ride passes are available on certain days. For a schedule call (800) 422–FAIR in-state or (816) 530–5600 out-of-state. More than 2,000 campsites are available on the fairgrounds. In addition to the state fair, the fairgrounds host numerous activities and events throughout the year, ranging from car races and sports tournaments to carnivals and concerts. For a schedule call (816) 826–0570.

This city was once a rugged frontier town and a terminal point for cattle drives. That rough heritage is celebrated during the **Rawhide Festival** in July. This festival features a mountain-man rendezvous, Native American cultural appreciation seminars and a powwow. You may witness a shootout or bank robbery during the festival. Call (816) 827–3103.

You can tour an American country estate at **Bothwell Lodge State Historic Site,** Highway 65. A local millionaire built a massive stone house between 1897 and 1928 on the side of a cliff. A guide takes you through the house pointing out the unusual design elements that reveal the idiosyncrasies of the owner, such as his separate, inaccessible three-story wing of the building. Small admission fee. Open Monday through Saturday 10:00 A.M. to 4:00 P.M., Sunday 12:00 to 5:00 P.M. The park has picnic facilities and a self-guided hiking trail that provides information about the property when it was the country getaway of John Bothwell. Call (816) 827–0510.

Sedalia is at the western end of the **Katy Trail State Park.** To reach the trailhead go north on Engineer Avenue, then turn east on Griessen Road to the park. For trail information and maps call (800) 334–6946.

Community theater productions are offered at **Liberty Center,** 111 West Fifth Street, in a restored 1920s theater building. The theater has a year-round schedule. Call (816) 827–3228.

KNOB NOSTER

Knob Noster State Park, Highway 132, offers a savannah landscape of prairie grasses and widely spaced trees. There is a visitor center with photographic displays and a naturalist on hand to answer your questions. The park has hiking and equestrian trails, several small lakes and a stream for fishing, and a wooded campground with seventy-three sites. Stop at the park office to find out about nature programs offered year-round. A map of an orienteering trail is also available. Call (816) 563–2463.

Once a year you can visit **Whiteman Air Force Base,** Highway 50, home of the Stealth Bomber. During an annual open house you can climb into older planes, view displays about aircraft and the Air Force, and see guard dogs, a mobile command station, and other military items. An air show and aerial demonstrations take place throughout the day. The open house is usually held in the summer, but it varies. To find out when it will be held, call (816) 687–1110.

WARRENSBURG

Central Missouri Repertory, on the campus of Central Missouri State University, offers three theater productions in July and August. One of them is geared toward children. For a schedule and ticket prices call (816) 543–4020.

Powell Gardens, Highway 50, is a relatively new, but beautiful, 800-acre botanical garden featuring demonstration gardens, native-plant landscapes, a twelve-acre lake, and several different types of specialty gardens.

Your children will enjoy walking through a wonderful wooded area that has wooden bridges spanning a babbling brook. The garden sponsors a full schedule of educational programs, many designed especially for children. Admission is $3.00 for adults, $1.00 for children ages twelve and younger, with a $10.00 family maximum. Open daily 9:00 A.M. to 5:00 P.M. Open until sunset April through October. Call (816) 566–2600.

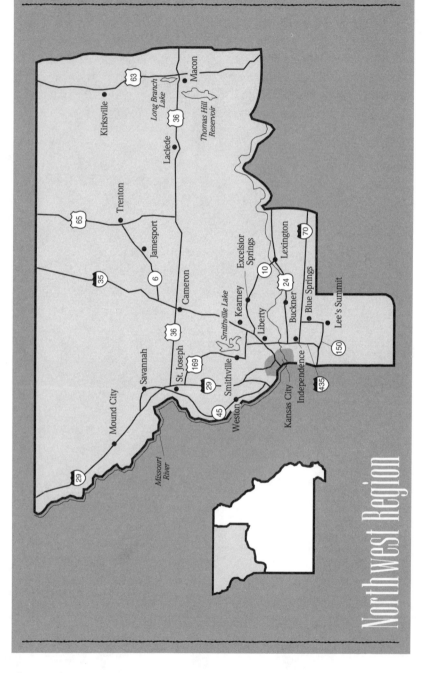

Northwest Region

Northwest Region

Although the northwestern region of the state is primarily rural, you'll find that Kansas City and the surrounding suburbs offer big-city fun with numerous first-class tourist attractions, big-league sports teams, and museums and historic sites of national importance. North of Kansas City, the Missouri River Valley is a major migratory flyway for waterfowl, bald eagles, and songbirds, providing ample opportunities for bird-watching and wildlife viewing. As you travel northeast in the region you'll find farms and small towns dotting the countryside, with abundant locations for outdoor recreation.

KANSAS CITY

This city, where east meets west, is known for great barbecue, jazz, and having more fountains than any city in the world except Rome. Although named for the neighboring state to the west, most of the city is in the state of Missouri. But any family looking for adventure shouldn't leave town without checking out what Kansas City has to offer on both sides of the state line. In addition to what you will find listed here, the city has many great things to see and do in the state of Kansas. For information about all attractions in the area, call (800) 767–7700.

Start your visit to the city with a ride on one of the **KC Trolleys** for an all-in-fun narrated tour of the city where you'll get jokes and silly stories along with the historical facts. You can stay on the trolley for a ninety-minute tour or get off anywhere along the route. Your tickets are good all day. Catch the trolley at **Crown Center,** 25th and Grand, or any one of fifteen other locations. Two different routes cover almost all the tourist attractions in the downtown area. Tickets, available from the drivers, are $4.00 for adults, $3.00 for children ages six to twelve. The trolleys run Monday through Saturday 10:00 A.M. to 10:00 P.M., Sunday 12:00 to 6:00 P.M. Closed in January and February. Call (816) 221–3399.

Crown Center, adjacent to the world headquarters of Hallmark Cards, offers shops, restaurants, theaters, and hotels in a splendid luxury setting. Entertainment is regularly provided on the lower level, and throughout the Christmas season musicians, puppeteers, and other seasonal entertainers perform. Your visit to this city wouldn't be complete without a stroll around the center. Open Monday through Saturday 10:00 A.M. to 6:00 P.M., Sunday 12:00 to 5:00 P.M.

The **Coterie Theater,** located on Level One at the center, offers a full season of delightful family theater productions from October through May. The performances are designed to be enjoyed by both children and adults. Tickets are $6.00 each. For a schedule, call (816) 474–6552. You can skate at the **Ice Terrace** in Crown Center Square from November to March. Admission is $4.00 for adults, $3.00 for children ages twelve and younger. Skate rental is $1.50. For hours call (816) 274–8411.

The **Hallmark Visitors Center** at Crown Center offers your family an opportunity to learn about the world's largest greeting-card company. There are fourteen exhibits ranging from memorabilia collected during eighty years in business, to clips of Hallmark Hall of Fame television dramas, to an automatic bow-making machine that turns out bows on demand. Your kids will love the room with 6-foot pencils, markers, brushes, paint tubes, and jars, where they can view a video illustrating how artists create greeting-card designs. Free admission. Open Monday through Friday 9:00 A.M. to 5:00 P.M., Saturday 9:30 A.M. to 4:30 P.M. Call (816) 274–5672.

Kaleidoscope, also part of the Hallmark Card facility, provides creative experiences for kids ages five to twelve. Parents are invited to stay, but you don't get to play like the kids do. You'll be put to work helping with the activities.

Factories that make cards, ribbon, wrapping paper, and party supplies have great stuff left over. It's bright, colorful, attractive, and the perfect fodder for fun. That is how this creative art experience center works. Kids are exposed to activities intended to stimulate their creative juices and then set loose with all that stuff left over from Hallmark factories. They get to cut, paste, tie, twist, color, draw—anything their little creative hearts desire. And the fun isn't over when it's time to go. Each child is given a paper bag to fill with ingredients to go. Don't let your kids miss this great experience. Free admission. Open on Saturday only. Pick up your tickets at 10:00 A.M. on the day you want to attend. Tickets are distributed on a first-come, first-served basis, so get there early. For information call (816) 274–8300.

While you're in town you have to eat some good barbecque, so check out one of the several locations of **Gates and Sons Bar-B-Q.** This original KC restaurant chain has been serving customers since 1945 and is considered one of the best barbecue purveyors in the country. You can get a hot and spicy version of their sauce, and the menu includes sandwiches, ribs, sausage, chicken, and mutton. For locations and hours call (816) 923–0900, or (816) 921–0409 after 5:00 P.M.

To really get a taste for the city's Western side, you have to visit the **American Royal Museum and Visitor Center,** 1701 American Royal Court. In the museum your children can sit on an English or Western saddle, weigh themselves on a livestock scale, play with farm items, see a film about the annual rodeo, and learn about the people who make the event so successful. Admission is $3.00 for adults, $2.00 for children ages two to twelve. Open Tuesday through Saturday 10:00 A.M. to 4:00 P.M., Sunday 12:00 to 4:00 P.M. Call (816) 221–9800.

The museum is a great stop at any time, but it's especially fun during November when the rodeo and livestock competitions are in full swing. The **American Royal Livestock, Horse Show and Rodeo** is one of the top twenty professional rodeos in the nation and draws contestants and spectators from all over. During the two-month season, the complex has a commercial trade show, a petting area with a variety of animals, and a full schedule of livestock shows, competitions, rodeos, and big-name entertainers. The event begins with the city's largest parade. Throughout the rest of the year, a wide variety of events and performers are scheduled at the complex and at **Kemper Arena,** which is right next door. For ticket prices and a schedule call (800) 821–5857 or (816) 221–7979.

Sports buffs can watch the **Kansas City Attack** professional indoor soccer team play at Kemper Arena from October through April. Tickets are $6.00 to $12.00. Call (816) 474–BALL. The **Kansas City Blades** professional ice hockey team also plays at Kemper from October through April. Tickets are $9.00 to $14.00, discounts available for kids seventeen and younger. Call (816) 842–1063.

Take your kids to the **City Market,** Fifth and Walnut, and show them what shopping centers looked like in years past. Here by the river in the area where the city began, more than 140 stalls offer everything from fresh produce to art and entertainment. On Saturday and Sunday, farmers come in from rural areas to sell their wares. Open Monday through Friday 9:00 A.M. to 4:00 P.M., Saturday 7:00 A.M. to 4:00 P.M., Sunday 10:00 A.M. to 4:00 P.M. Call (816) 842–1271.

While you're at the market be sure to tour the ***Arabia* Steamboat Museum.** Finding buried treasure is a common childhood fantasy, and at this museum your children can learn the fascinating details of a real-life treasure hunt. You can meet the treasure hunters and see their spoils displayed in 30,000 square feet of exhibit space.

In 1856 the steamboat *Arabia* hit a log snag while steaming up the Missouri River and sank in 15 feet of water, taking her 200-ton frontier cargo with her. But the river changed course and that sunken steamboat ended up buried in a farmer's field. From 1988 to 1989, five families excavated the steamboat from underneath 45 feet of mud. The recovered treasure comprises the largest collection of pre–Civil War artifacts in existence. You can study the contents of this time capsule from the American frontier and talk to one of the hardworking and determined people who performed the salvage operation and preserved the artifacts. Admission is $5.50 for adults, $3.75 for children ages four to twelve; ages three and younger are free. Open Monday through Saturday 10:00 A.M. to 6:00 P.M., Sunday 12:00 to 5:00 P.M. Call (816) 471–4030.

Penn Valley Park, on Pershing Road between Main Street and Southwest Boulevard provides several overlooks where you can get a great view of the city skyline and use the picnic facilities. Or you can get a free breathtaking view of the city from the thirtieth-floor **City Hall Observation Deck,** 414 East 12th Street. Open Monday through Friday 8:30 A.M. to 4:15 P.M. Call (816) 274–2222.

Maple Woods Natural Area, located just north of downtown, is an eighteen-acre oasis of stately old-growth forest. The dense tree canopy offers tranquil hiking trails for observing songbirds, rabbits, squirrels, deer, foxes and wildflowers. Take Highway 169 north, turn east on Barry Road, turn south on North Oak, then turn east on NE 76th Street for 1½ miles. For hours or information call (816) 436–2200.

Even if you think the **Federal Reserve Bank of Kansas City,** 925 Grand Boulevard, is too complex and will bore your children, give it a try. The display in the mezzanine of the bank is great for all ages. Kids can compare real and counterfeit money, see a twenty-seven-pound gold bar, examine money from other countries, and learn how much a Happy Meal costs in seven different countries. A multimedia computer program lets you test your skill as chairman of the Federal Reserve Board, and an automated teller machine spits out real receipts and lets little ones play with something usually reserved for grownups. If you call in advance you can get a one-hour tour of the bank itself. The best part comes at the end of your visit when you receive a small bag of money, unfortunately shredded beyond any hope of ever using it. Free admission. Open Monday through Friday 8:00 A.M. to 5:00 P.M. Call (816) 881–2554. Older kids may enjoy visiting the **Kansas City Board of Trade,** 4800 Main Street, to watch the trading of Value Line stock index futures as well as the world's largest winter-wheat futures market. Free third-floor observation deck is open Monday through Friday 8:15 A.M. to 3:30 P.M. (816) 753–7500.

The **Kansas City Museum,** 3218 Gladstone Boulevard, is a wonderful combination of history and science museum, housed in a luxury turn-of-the-century mansion and several buildings on the surrounding grounds. Your kids will have a great time as they explore interactive displays and hands-on exhibits that tell about the early history of the Kansas City area and explain about the weather, the forces of nature that affect us, and other scientific concepts. On the lower level you'll find a replica of a 1910 drugstore complete with a soda fountain selling ice cream treats and old-fashioned phosphates. The museum has a year-long schedule of special events and learning activities to promote history and science. Admission is $2.50 for adults, $2.00 for children ages three to seventeen. Open Tuesday through Saturday 9:30 A.M. to 4:30 P.M., Sunday 12:00 to 4:30 P.M. Call (816) 483–8300.

The **Challenger Learning Center** behind the museum provides real-istic simulations of space flights, with visitors manning the controls. The simulator is modeled after NASA's Johnson Space Center. Don't miss an out-of-this-world experience in space—make your reservations in advance. Family missions for adults and children ages six and older take place on Saturday and Sunday, with expanded missions during school holidays. Tickets are $5.00 per person. A planetarium provides astronomy shows for various age groups. Tickets are $3.50 per person. Call (816) 483–5610.

Baseball fans will enjoy a visit to the **Negro Leagues Baseball Museum,** 18th and Vine Streets. It's located in the heart of the historic jazz district and chronicles the history and heroes of Negro League baseball from its origin after the Civil War, to its demise in the 1960s. Small admission charge. Open Tuesday through Saturday 10:00 A.M. to 4:30 P.M., Sunday 12:00 to 4:30 P.M. Call (816) 221–1920.

If airplanes, especially propeller-driven transport craft, are of interest to you or someone in your family, visit **Save A Connie, Inc.** at the downtown airport, 480 NW Richards Road. This small esoteric museum tells the story of early aircraft with photographs, artifacts, and two restored aircraft; a Lockheed Constellation and a Martin 404. Donations are requested. For hours call (816) 421–3401.

You can take a look at history from a child's point of view at the **Toy and Miniature Museum,** 5235 Oak Street. You'll see miniatures, toys, dolls, and dollhouses from years past. Admission is $3.00 for adults, $2.50 for ages thirteen to eighteen, $1.50 for ages five through twelve, free for children under five. For hours call (816) 333–2055.

Country Club Plaza—or as locals call it, the Plaza—is a great place for both serious shoppers and those who just want to window-shop or take a walk. This elegant 14-square block area, located off Ward Parkway, is filled with specialty stores and restaurants. The area also sports so much great architecture and art that it brings to mind an Old World European city and could be considered an outdoor public art gallery. Get a brochure with a map of the fountains, sculptures, and murals, many portraying children, and go on a walking treasure hunt to find your favorites. Or you can catch a ride in a horse-drawn carriage for a thoroughly delightful experience. Look for the red ticket booth outside Seville on the Plaza, 500

The Challenger Learning Center at the Kansas City Museum lets adults and children participate in simulated space flight training. (Courtesy Kansas City Museum)

Nichols Road. Rides are offered daily. Stores are open Monday through Saturday 10:00 A.M. to 7:00 P.M., Sunday 12:00 to 5:00 P.M. For map or information call (816) 753–0100.

Don't miss the plaza during the Christmas season. At 7:00 P.M. on Thanksgiving, a lighting ceremony marks the beginning of the season, and the lights are turned on at 7:30 P.M. Until mid-January the entire area is lit by miles and miles of multicolored lights. During this time the shops are open later in the evening and the atmosphere is enchanting.

You'll find two excellent art museums in the city, the **Nelson-Atkins Museum,** 4525 Oak Street, and **Kemper Museum of Contemporary Art,** 4420 Warwick Avenue. The Nelson-Atkins is considered one of the finest general art museums in the country. Children will be most interested in the cloister from a medieval French church, the knight in full parade dress, the modern sculpture room, authentic Chinese temple, and the rooms furnished with Oriental furniture. Admission is $4.00 for adults, $1.00 for students ages six to eighteen; children ages five and younger are free. Call (816) 561–4000. Pick up a map and you can walk around the seventeen-acre sculpture garden on the museum grounds. Kids will enjoy seeing the artwork, the most noticeable being the four giant badminton shuttlecocks on the lawn.

At the Kemper Museum of Contemporary Art your children can see what today's artists are creating. Free admission. Call (816) 561–3737. Both art museums are open Tuesday through Saturday 10:00 A.M. to 4:00 P.M., Friday evenings until 9:00 P.M., Saturday evenings until 5:00 P.M., and Sunday 1:00 to 5:00 P.M.

The historic **Westport** area, Broadway Boulevard and Westport Road, was the jumping-off point for settlers leaving on the Santa Fe, California, and Oregon Trails. Today it's an entertainment area with unique small shops and restaurants where it's fun to stroll.

There are always plenty of music, dance, and theater productions suitable for families throughout the city. The **American Heartland Theater** in Crown Center puts on Broadway plays and musicals. The **State Ballet of Missouri** has an annual production of *The Nutcracker* and the Missouri Repertory Theater performs *A Christmas Carol* every holiday season. The **Folly Theater,** in a historic 12th Street building, offers a children's sampler series of productions. For recorded information on live productions and other events in the KC area, call (816) 691–3800.

The Missouri Repertory Theatre presents the **Dickens Holiday Fair** at the Municipal Auditorium during December. Dickens's London comes to life with food and entertainment from that period. A marketplace offers the wares of artisans, and performers provide family entertainment throughout the event. For dates and ticket prices call (816) 889–STAR, ext. 4267.

Beautiful **Swope Park,** 6601 Swope Parkway, is one of the largest municipal parks in the country, with 1,769 acres. You'll find picnic and athletic facilities, as well as the Blue River winding through the park and Lake of the Woods stocked with sun perch, bass, crappie, and catfish for fishing enthusiasts. During the holiday season the park features a display of lights. For information call (816) 363–7800. **Starlight Theater,** an 8,000-seat outdoor theater, in the middle of the park, offers family entertainment including Broadway musicals and concerts by top national performers during the summer months. For a schedule and ticket prices call (816) 363–7827.

The **Kansas City Zoological Gardens,** in Swope Park, covers 202 acres and is a zoo on the move. An Australia area opened in 1993, and a ninety-five-acre Africa exhibit went on display in 1995. The newest attraction at the zoo is the Deramus Education Pavilion, which has interactive exhibits, films, and an IMAX theater.

The Australia area offers a five-minute film, a working sheep station, and opportunities to get close to kangaroos, dingos, emus, and kookaburras. The Africa exhibit includes a seventeen-acre plains area, an eight-acre forest, and individual areas for chimpanzees, gorillas, cheetahs, lions, and rhinos. This large-scale re-creation of animal habitats in Kenya, Tanzania, Uganda, and Zaire makes you feel as if you have been transported to Africa. These exhibits attempt to be as realistic as possible and may require some patience and searching before you spot the animals. Authentic vegetation is incorporated into the exhibits, and the landscaping is an integral part of the immersion experience. An eleven-acre lake offers paddleboat and safari-boat rides.

An exhibit called the Okavango Elephant Sanctuary provides a natural habitat without any bars separating you and the elephants. The "International Festival" and "Farmland in the USA" exhibits enable you to see exotic and domesticated animals up close. Train, camel, and pony rides are available in various locations. Presentations of birds, mammals, and reptiles take place throughout the zoo. Admission is $5.00 for adults, $2.50 for children ages two to eleven. The zoo is free from 9:00 to 11:00 A.M. on Tuesday. Parking is $2.00. Open daily 9:00 A.M. to 5:00 P.M. Zoo closes at 4:00 P.M. October 15 to March 30. Call (816) 871–5700.

For a wonderfully intimate look at flora and fauna, don't miss the **Lakeside Nature Center** located in the park. This center rehabilitates injured wildlife, conducts environmental education programs and maintains the exhibits focusing on native species and wildlife. The staff and volunteers offer hands-on activities for children and are always willing to seize a "teachable moment" with visitors. Nature trails near the center provide visitors with a view of natural areas in the park. Free admission. Open Tuesday through Saturday 9:00 A.M. to 5:00 P.M. Call (816) 444–4656.

For a country experience without leaving the city, visit **Benjamin Ranch,** 6401 E. 87th Street. Located on the historic Santa Fe Trail, this working Western ranch provides barn parties, hayrides, Western entertainment, country-western dancing and lessons, stagecoach rides, and horse and pony rides. Every July Fourth weekend, the ranch hosts the **Kansas City Jaycees ProRodeo.** The event lasts for four days and includes children's activities, a petting zoo, craft booths, and fireworks. There is a Ramada Inn on the site with 250 rooms for guests who want to stay for a while. Call (800) 2–RAMADA or (816) 765–1100 for rates and reservations.

The **Cave Springs Interpretive Center,** 8701 Gregory Boulevard, is located on a site that was once a stopover on the Sante Fe Trail. The center features changing exhibits on the nature and history of the area and has several trails leading to a cave, a spring and various wildlife habitats. Admission is $1.00. Open Tuesday through Saturday 10:00 A.M. to 5:00 P.M. Call (816) 358–2283.

LEE'S SUMMIT

The Kansas City suburbs have spread out to encompass a ring of historic small towns that offer numerous attractions for families. In the southeast suburbs are several lakes and nature preserves. **Longview Lake,** located in Longview Lake Park on Raytown Road, offers 930 acres for powerboating, waterskiing, jet-skiing, or pontoon boating. Fishing is also popular here and includes bluegill, carp, channel cat, largemouth bass, walleye, and crappie. A full-service marina offers boat rental, marine supplies, bait, and tackle. The lake has a sand beach with volleyball facilities. Also in the park are playground equipment, picnic facilities, a 7-mile asphalt lakeside bike path, and campgrounds. **Christmas in the Park,** at the park campgrounds, features an elaborate drive-through lighting display with more than 225,000 lights and 175 animated scenes. Donations are requested. Open from Thanksgiving through December. Call (816) 795–8200.

BLUE SPRINGS

Fleming Park, south of Highway 70 on Woods Chapel Road, has three lakes and offers a wealth of recreation opportunities. Regulations limiting the horsepower of the boats allowed on **Lake Jacomo** make it perfect for sailboat and pontoon-boat enthusiasts. A full-service marina provides boat rental and marine and fishing supplies. Powerboaters can enjoy nearby **Blue Springs Lake,** with a sand beach for sunbathers and swimmers. Small Prairie Lake and the two larger lakes are all excellent fishing locations.

> ## JANE'S TOP FAMILY ADVENTURES IN THE NORTHWEST REGION
>
> 1. Kansas City Zoological Park, Kansas City, (816) 871–5700
> 2. American Royal Museum and Visitors Center, Kansas City, (816) 221–9800
> 3. Arabia Steamboat Museum, Kansas City, (816) 471–4030
> 4. Kaleidoscope and Hallmark Visitors Center, Kansas City, (816) 274–5672
> 5. Worlds of Fun, Oceans of Fun, Liberty, (816) 454–4545
> 6. Pony Express National Memorial, St. Joseph, (800) 530–5930 or (816) 279–5059
> 7. Swan Creek Nature Preserve, Mound City, (816) 442–3187

In the park don't miss **Kemper Outdoor Education Center.** Wildlife feeding stations attract white-tailed deer, wild turkeys, and songbirds for visitors to observe. Inside, your kids will love seeing—and in some cases touching—displays of reptiles, amphibians, and native fish. The grounds offer nature trails and a beautiful water garden with Japanese koi. Free admission. Open Monday through Friday 8:00 A.M. to 4:00 P.M., Saturday and Sunday 12:00 to 4:00 P.M. During the winter call for hours. Call (816) 229–8980.

Fleming Park includes several marked nature trails and campgrounds for tent and RV camping. An archery range in the park boasts three scenic shooting trails and hosts several tournaments each year. A paved airstrip for radio-controlled model airplanes and a small lake for radio-controlled boats are also available. Call (816) 795–8200.

You and your children will enjoy strolling through **Missouri Town 1855,** also located in Fleming Park. More than thirty old houses and other authentic buildings have been moved to this location to re-create a typical 1850s farming community. Costumed craftsmen, guides, and musicians portray the lives of early settlers in the six-block community and provide information to anyone interested in learning about that time in history. Admission is $3.00 for adults, $2.00 for children ages five to thirteen. Open Wednesday through Sunday 9:00 A.M. to 4:30 P.M. April 15 to November 15. Open weekends only during the winter months. Call (816) 795–8200, ext. 1-260.

Across the road is a native hoofed-animal enclosure where bison and elk roam freely. An observation tower lets you watch the animals from on high. You can take a tour inside the enclosure on a hay-filled truck for a small fee on Saturdays from April through October. Bring apples or pears to feed the animals. Tickets must be purchased the day of the tour. Call (816) 229–8980.

The nature lovers of your family can get more information and enjoyment at **Burr Oak Woods Conservation Nature Center,** 1401 NW Park Road. This great center offers hands-on, interactive exhibits explaining the flora and fauna of the KC area. Multimedia programs allow kids to make decisions about the environment and see the results immediately. The center regularly schedules special programs, concerts and performances for children and adults. The facility is surrounded by more than 1,000 acres of state forest with several interpretive hiking trails and picnic facilities. Free admission. Open Tuesday through Saturday 9:00 A.M. to 5:00 P.M., Sunday 12:00 to 5:00 P.M. For a schedule of special events or for other information call (816) 228–3766.

INDEPENDENCE

Directly east of the downtown area, this frontier boomtown once served settlers heading west. Take the Blue Ridge Cutoff exit from Highway 70 and you can stop at the **Missouri Tourist Information Center,** to collect information about attractions all over the state. Call (816) 861–8800.

This town played an important role in the history of westward expansion, and you can explore that period, which lasted from 1820 to 1855, at the **National Frontier Trails Center,** 318 Pacific Avenue. You can see two authentic pioneer wagons, learn about the trades and businesses that prepared emigrants for the journey, view a seventeen-minute film documenting this great exodus, and examine artifacts found along the trails. Admission is $2.50 for adults, $1.00 for children ages ten to seventeen; children ages nine and younger are free. Open Monday through Saturday 9:00 A.M. to 4:30 P.M., Sunday 12:30 to 4:30 P.M. from April through October. From November through March the center is open Monday through Friday 10:00 A.M. to 4:00 P.M. and weekends 12:30 to 4:00 P.M. Call (816) 325–7575. **Santa-Cali-Gon Days** is held on Labor Day weekend and celebrates the pioneer heritage of this town. The festival includes entertainment, an interpretive area with demonstrations, and food and crafts booths. All activities take place in Independence Square. Call (816) 252–4745.

See the jail where outlaws Frank James and William Quantrill were held while awaiting trial. The **1859 Jail, Marshal's Home and Museum,** 217 North Main Street, has been authentically restored to provide a chilling look at frontier justice in the mid-1800s. Admission is $3.00 for adults, $1.00 for children ages six to sixteen. Open Monday through Saturday 10:00 A.M. to 5:00 P.M., Sunday 1:00 to 4:00 P.M. April through October. From November through March open Tuesday through Saturday 10:00 A.M. to 4:00 P.M. and Sunday 11:00 A.M. to 4:00 P.M. Call (816) 252–1892.

This is also the hometown of President Harry S Truman, and there are several sites associated with the president preserved by the National Park Service. The **Harry S Truman Library and Museum** documents the career of this popular president. It houses a replica of the Oval Office as it looked during Truman's presidency, and numerous photographs and artifacts from that time. The house Truman and his wife owned during his presidency is open for tours, and you can see his law office and the courtroom where he presided as a county judge at the **Jackson County Courthouse.** Start your visit to the Truman sites at the **Truman Home Ticket and Information Center,** Truman Road and Main Street, right on historic Independence Square. Here you can get tickets, join a tour group, and view a free twelve-minute introductory slide program. Open daily 8:30 A.M. to 5:00 P.M. Call (816) 254–7199.

The **Reorganized Church of Jesus Christ of Latter-Day Saints Auditorium and Temple,** River Boulevard and West Walnut Street, is open to the public and provides tours. Free organ recitals on one of the largest church organs in the country are performed in the auditorium daily at 3:00 P.M. from June through August and on Sunday during the rest of the year. Call (816) 833–1000, ext. 2100. The **Children's Peace Pavilion** on the campus is the only museum in the world devoted to encouraging peace. Children can play games, listen to recorded stories of children's accomplishments, create arts and crafts projects, and make music by running through a series of colored lights. The interactive exhibits are designed for ages five through twelve. Free admission. For hours call (816) 521–3033. The **Mormon Visitors' Center,** 937 West Walnut Street, presents the history of the religion with interactive video displays, paintings, and artifacts. Call (816) 836–3466.

You'll find four beautifully landscaped miniature golf courses, a 7,000-square-foot game center with all the latest video games, and an exotic bird exhibit with more than eighty birds, all in a five-acre park setting at **Cool Crest,** 10735 East Highway 40. Call (816) 358–0088.

Independence is the home of Kansas City's major-league sports complex, located at the Blue Ridge Cutoff exit off Highway 70. The **Kansas City Royals** baseball team plays at Kauffman Stadium, and ticket prices range from $9.00 to $14.00. Toddlers who can walk underneath the turnstile are admitted free. For dates and availability call (800) 422–1969.

The **Kansas City Chiefs** play right next door in Arrowhead Stadium. If football is your family's idea of a good time, you have plenty of company in this region. The Kansas City area and much of the northern part of the state is Chiefs territory, and you'll see the signature red and white, arrowhead-emblazoned jackets on young and old alike. Tickets to Chiefs games range from $20 to $35. Call (816) 924–9400.

When hunger strikes you can visit **Clinton's Old Fashioned Soda Fountain,** 100 West Maple Avenue, or **Tommy's Old Fashioned Ice Cream and Deli,** 121 West Lexington Avenue, and introduce your children to ice cream treats served the old-fashioned way, from a real soda fountain.

BUCKNER

Head east on Highway 24, then turn north on Highway 20–E, and on a high bluff overlooking the Missouri River you'll find **Fort Osage,** founded in 1808 by William Clark, co-commander of the Lewis and Clark expedition. You can see several reconstructed buildings including a blockhouse, officers' quarters, and soldiers' barracks. A visitor center and costumed interpreters help you journey back to the time of 1812 when this fort was part of a federally controlled fur-trading system. Small admission fee. Open Wednesday through Sunday 9:00 A.M. to 4:30 P.M. from April 15 through November 15. Open weekends only during the rest of the year. Call (816) 795–8200.

Visit **Osage Honey Farms, Inc.,** 222 Santa Fe, to view bees at work and buy some of the pure, unfiltered honey produced here. A glass-enclosed hive lets you see the bees in action. For hours call (816) 650–5637.

LEXINGTON

This small historic town has more than 100 antebellum homes and buildings, which can be toured on foot or in your car. Northwest of town you'll find the **Battle of Lexington State Historic Site,** 10th and Utah Streets, where a visitor center explains the details of the major Civil War battle fought here. You can take a mile-long, self-guided walking tour of the battlefield, where the earthworks and trenches are still clearly visible, or fish in the Missouri River, which runs along the park. For maps and information call (816) 259–4654. You can also visit the **1830s Log House** on Main Street, a living-history museum restored to reflect family life during the early 1800s. For directions and information call (816) 259–3082.

East of town in the fertile Missouri River valley, take a scenic country drive along Highway 24, the route of the Santa Fe Trail. There are many small orchards and farms in this area, so watch for signs directing you to seasonal roadside markets and you-pick-it operations. During the spring you'll find asparagus, strawberries, and bedding plants. Summertime brings blueberries, blackberries, peaches, tomatoes, and sweet corn. In the autumn you'll find apples, cider, pumpkins, gourds, peppers, and mums. The holiday season offers Christmas trees, wreaths, greenery, and winter apples.

EXCELSIOR SPRINGS

At the end of the nineteenth century, this small town gained fame as a spa offering naturally occurring mineral water to visitors from all over the world. The **Fishing River,** a system of parks and trails that winds through the town following the creek and mineral springs, is a reminder of that past. This area includes hiking trails, playground equipment, picnic facilities, and the Superior Spring and Pagoda, the last of thirty-five wells that once supplied mineral water to visitors. If you wish, you can still get a mineral water massage at the **Hall of Waters,** 201 East Broadway, or stay at **The Elms Resort Hotel,** Regent and Elms Boulevard. This luxury hotel has been serving visitors since 1888 and can boast famous and infamous guests from Harry S Truman to Al Capone. Call (816) 637–1040.

LIBERTY

The charming downtown square in this small suburb north of Kansas City is where you can start your explorations. Stop at the Liberty Area Chamber of Commerce, 9 S. Leonard Street, to pick up tourist information and maps of local historic districts and attractions. Open Monday through Friday 8:30 A.M. to 5:30 P.M. Call (816) 781–5200. At the **Historic Liberty Jail,** 216 N. Main Street, you can take a free tour of the 1833 jail where Mormon president and prophet Joseph Smith was imprisoned. Open daily 9:00 A.M. to 9:00 P.M. Call (816) 781–3188. The **Jesse James Bank Museum,** 103 Water Street, was the site of a daylight bank robbery attributed to Jesse James and his gang. The bank and vault have been restored to their 1866 condition. Small admission charge. Open Monday through Saturday 9:00 A.M. to 4:00 P.M., Sunday 12:00 to 4:00 P.M. Call (816) 781–4458. The **Clay County Museum,** 14 North Main Street, is housed in an authentic nineteenth-century drugstore and includes artifacts and exhibits from the drugstore, the town newspaper, and a doctor's office, as well as numerous items from everyday life in the 1800s. Small admission charge. Open Tuesday through Saturday 1:00 to 4:00 P.M. Call (816) 792–1849. On Saturday from May through October you'll find the **Liberty Farmers' Market,** on the west side of the square, offering a variety of produce, flowers, and bedding plants for sale. Call (816) 781–5105.

For those seeking more modern diversions, you can find first-class amusement-park excitement at **Worlds of Fun,** Highway 435, exit 54. The more than 140 rides, shows, and attractions have an international theme based on Jules Verne's *Around the World in Eighty Days*. You'll find the Timber Wolf, one of the top-ranked roller coasters in the country; the Orient Express, the nation's largest steel roller coaster; and several popular water rides. If you have small kids, head for Pandemonium, an area with

Le Carrousel is one of the 140 rides, shows, and attractions at Worlds of Fun.
(Courtesy Worlds of Fun)

special rides for little ones. Admission is $24.95 for adults and children over 48 inches tall, $4.95 for children older than age three and shorter than 48 inches. Children three and younger are free. Open daily 10:30 A.M. to dark May through August, and weekends only during late April, September, and early October. For information call (816) 454–4545.

Fun of the wet and wild variety is available at sixty-acre **Oceans of Fun,** adjacent to the amusement park. This water park offers thirty-five attractions including a million-gallon wave pool for body surfing and rafting, children's water playgrounds, giant water slides, and an adults-only pool with a swim-up refreshment cabana. Admission is $16.95 for adults and children over 48 inches tall, $4.95 for children older than age three and shorter than 48 inches. Open daily late May through early September from 10:00 A.M. to dark. Combination tickets for both parks are available. For information call (816) 454–4545.

You can step back into the past at **Shoal Creek,** 7000 NE Barry Road, a living-history museum comprised of seventeen period structures and located in Hodge Park. You may see native Missouri elk, deer, foxes, or bison in the park. There is a self-guided tour of the park, or you can come during special events to get a more structured experience with costumed interpreters showing you the way things used to be. Free daily admission, small fee during special events. Open Monday through Friday 9:00 A.M. to 3:00 P.M. Call (816) 792–2655.

KEARNEY

You're in Jesse James country now, so tour the **Jesse James Farm and Museum,** where Jesse and his brother, Frank, grew up during the mid-1800s. Take Highway 92 east then north on Jesse James Farm Road. Admission is $3.00 for adults, $1.00 for children ages six to twelve. Open daily 9:00 A.M. to 4:00 P.M. May through September. From October to April closed until noon on Saturday and Sunday. Call (816) 635–6065. An outdoor drama based on the life of Jesse James is performed during the summer season. Tickets are $8.00 to $13.00. For information call (816) 792–7691.

East of town at **Watkins Mill State Park** (follow Highway 92 to Highway RA), you'll find recreational facilities and several historic buildings open for visitors. The park has more than 100 campsites, modern rest-room facilities, picnic areas, hiking and biking trails, and a small lake for fishing and swimming. Part of this 1,000-acre park was once a bustling plantation, and you can tour several buildings left from that era: the Watkins Woolen Mill (with the original machinery), the Watkins home, a church, a school, and several smaller buildings. Small admission fee. For hours call (816) 296–3357. For park information call (816) 296–3387.

SMITHVILLE

Just north of this small town is **Smithville Lake,** one of the newest large man-made lakes in the state. There are three recreation areas on the lake featuring more than 700 campsites, two swimming beaches with rest-room facilities, 200 picnic areas, and two full-service marinas where you can rent a boat or find services for your own boat. There is also a special launching area for the exclusive use of sailboaters. Visit the **Jerry L. Litton Visitor Center,** located off Highway 92 on Highway DD, to learn about this Corps of Engineers project and get information on the area. No admission fee. Open Monday through Friday 8:00 A.M. to 4:00 P.M. Call (816) 532–0174.

There are three horseback-riding and hiking trails in the lake area, accessible from the **Crows Creek** area, Highway E. For information call (816) 532–0174. The **Kansas City Trapshooters Association** main-tains a public shooting park off Highway W in the **Camp Branch** area, with trap and skeet fields overlooking the lake. Call (816) 532–4427. **Smith's Fork Park Campground,** on Highway DD, is a complete family recreational facility with campsites, a go-cart track, batting cages, an archery range, spillway fishing area, and a golf driving range. Live enter-tainment, provided throughout the summer in an outdoor amphitheater, includes country and bluegrass music, fireworks and theater productions. Call (816) 532–1023.

Fishing tournaments and sailboat races are regularly scheduled at this 7,200-acre lake, which is well suited to these diversions. An annual **Lake Festival** is held the first of August, with live entertainment, a carnival, pony rides, demonstrations, food booths, a parade, and many other family events. For information on any of the recreation areas or events at the lake call (816) 532–0803.

WESTON

Every fall the **Applefest Celebration** is held the first of October in this small historic town. You can press your own apple cider and sample delicious apple treats, the most popular being the apple dumplings. Vendors provide a variety of other food, and your family can watch dancers, listen to musicians, and participate in free hands-on children's activities. Several nearby farms sell apples and host other family activities. For a schedule of events and list of attractions to visit in town call (816) 640–2909.

Wintertime outdoor fun is available at **Snow Creek Ski Area,** Highway 45, where you will find nine intermediate and two beginner ski runs served by two triple-chair lifts and three rope tows. Artificial snow is provided when Mother Nature doesn't oblige, so skiing runs from mid-December to mid-March. Rental equipment and lessons at all levels are available. For hours of operation and prices call (816) 386–2200. For snow report call (816) 589–SNOW.

Highway 45 offers a scenic drive along the river and many opportunities to enjoy nature. This road follows the Missouri River and passes several parks and natural areas where you can stop for outdoor recreation. **Weston Bend State Park,** located 1 mile south of town off Highway 45, is adjacent to the river and has picnic facilities, a campground, and hiking and biking trails. Access to the river for fishing is also provided. Call (816) 386–5443.

If your family enjoys watching wildlife, visit **Little Bean Marsh Conservation Area,** located off Highway 45 north of town. This small marsh along the river was mentioned in the journals of Lewis and Clark for the abundance of wildlife here. You can still see various songbirds, bitterns, rails, and herons in the sloughs and backwaters. A viewing tower provides a panoramic look at the area and is a great place to watch waterfowl, bald eagles, and marsh hawks during winter months.

Another preserved habitat close by is **Bluffwoods Conservation Area.** Take Highway 59 to County Road 219, then follow the signs to the area. These 2,000 acres are a remnant of the lush forests that once grew along the Missouri River. Watch for birds, raccoons, deer, foxes, rabbits, and opossum in the deep woods and open ridges. At the southwest end of the area you'll find Lone Pine Trail, which leads you to a spectacular view of the river valley. Picnic areas and primitive campsites are available here. For information about either area call (816) 271–3100.

Nearby, **Lewis and Clark State Park,** on Highway 138, offers more variety in outdoor recreation. You can fish, swim, canoe, or waterski on the 365-acre Sugar Lake. Modern camping and picnic facilities are available. Call (816) 579–5564.

ST. JOSEPH

Like several other small cities in the state, this one has taken a small claim to fame and turned it into a great tourist experience. This is the city that launched the Pony Express. For the short span of eighteen months, riders took off from a small stable downtown and rode approximately 2,000 miles west to deliver the mail to Sacramento, California. You can obtain information about the Pony Express sites, as well as other attractions around the city, by visiting the Pony Express Regional Tourist Information Center Caboose, 4016 Frederick Boulevard. Open Monday through Saturday 9:00 A.M. to 5:00 P.M., April through September. For tourist information call (800) 785–0360 or (816) 232–6688.

Catch the **First Street Trolley** at one of several local hotels or at the center of town and ride all day, getting off at any of the ten museums downtown. Or just stay on the trolley and ride the one-hour circuit for a great tour of the city. An all-day pass is $2.50 for adults, $1.25 for seniors and children ages six to eighteen; ages six and younger are free. Single-trip fares are less than $1.00 per rider. Trolley operates Monday through Saturday 10:00 A.M. to 6:00 P.M., May through October. Call (800) 785–0360 or (816) 233–6688.

When you visit the **Pony Express National Memorial,** 914 Penn Street, you can relive the moment when a rider named Johnny Fry waited anxiously atop his horse, Sylph, for a cannon to sound the signal to begin the first run of the Pony Express. The museum is housed in the original Pike's Peak Stables, and you can pump water from the same well that was used to water the horses. It's a great museum for children, who can sit on a wooden sawhorse equipped with a saddle and handle an authentic reproduction of the mochilas (saddlebags) that carried the mail, or walk inside a typical relay station situated along the route. A diorama with special effects re-creates the desert air, mountain cold, and some of the smells encountered along the riders' trips between Missouri and California. Twenty-one interactive exhibits allow visitors to experience every aspect of this glorious experiment, from choosing horses suitable for the trip to tapping out messages on a telegraph, the invention that put the Pony Express operation out of business. Admission is $3.00 for adults, $2.50 for seniors, $1.00 for children ages seven to eighteen; ages six and younger are free. Open Monday through Saturday 9:00 A.M. to 5:00 P.M. and Sunday 1:00 to 5:00 P.M. From June through September the museum is open until 6:00 P.M. Call (800) 530–5930 or (816) 279–5059.

The headquarters of the company that operated the Pony Express, the Central Overland California and Pike's Peak Express Company, is located just a few blocks away from the stables. The **Patee House Museum,** 12th and Penn Streets, was once an elegant 140-room hotel. Now the building is a wonderful and strange conglomeration of nooks and crannies filled with artifacts and antiques from the town's past. It seems that the people in this city don't throw anything away—they just donate it to the Patee House. If you or your children can't find anything interesting here, you're not trying.

In addition to the restored Pony Express headquarters office, there's a row of simulated storefronts from the late 1800s called the "Streets of St. Joe," featuring a general store, a photographer's studio, a daguerreotype shop, a Victorian home, a dentist's office, a jail chronicling a century of crime, an optical shop, and several horse-drawn vehicles. The museum also houses a full-size steam engine you can climb into, old radios and telephones, tools, quilts, furniture, clothes, a room full of mechanized toys, and thousands of artifacts too numerous to mention. Don't leave without visiting the old-fashioned Buffalo Saloon in the train depot, where you can get soft drinks and popcorn. Plan on spending an hour or longer in the museum—there's plenty to see. Admission is $2.00 for adults, $1.00 for children ages six to eighteen; ages five and younger are free. Open Monday through Saturday 10:00 A.M. to 5:00 P.M., Sunday 1:00 to 5:00 P.M. April through October. Open only on Saturday and Sunday from November to March. Call (816) 232–8206.

Behind the massive Patee House Museum is the tiny four-room **Jesse James Home,** the house where fellow gang member Bob Ford shot the famous outlaw from behind to collect a $10,000 reward. It's a tiny but intriguing place. You can see the hole in the wall where the bullet lodged after passing through its victim, the gouges in the floor where souvenir seekers took pieces of blood-stained wood to sell, and photographs and information about the James family and Jesse's lawless career. Small admission fee. Open Monday through Saturday 10:00 A.M. to 4:00 P.M. and Sunday 1:00 to 4:00 P.M. From June through August the home is open until 5:00 P.M. Call (816) 232–8206.

The stately and dignified **St. Joseph Museum,** 1100 Charles Street, is located in a magnificent Gothic mansion built in 1879. The museum documents the history of the city and also features an extensive Native American collection, including totem poles, kayaks, and articles of clothing. A local-history section details the important role the city played in the development of the American West and has a replica of city founder Joseph Robidoux's fur-trading post.

Your children will enjoy following the painted footprints on the floor to find stuffed animals and birds in the natural-history area. You'll find numerous dioramas of the flora and fauna of the Midwest from pre-settlement times to the present.

If you have young children, don't miss the "Touch and Go Room" where kids can load small sacks and boxes onto a half-scale covered wagon, climb a miniature log fort, or sit inside a small tepee. Binoculars are provided for kids or adults who want a close-up look at the birds crowding the outside feeding stations. Inside is a live bullsnake named Stretch. Admission is $2.00 for adults, $1.00 for children ages seven to eighteen; ages six and younger are free. Open Monday through Saturday 9:00 A.M. to 5:00 P.M. and Sunday 1:00 to 5:00 P.M. Call (816) 232–8471.

The **Albrecht-Kemper Museum of Art,** 2818 Frederick Boulevard, has a fine collection of eighteenth-, nineteenth-, and twentieth-century American art, including works by Missouri artists George Caleb Bingham and Thomas Hart Benton. Admission is $3.00 for adults, $1.00 for students ages twelve to eighteen; ages eleven and younger are free. Open Tuesday through Saturday 10:00 A.M. to 4:00 P.M. and Sunday 1:00 to 4:00 P.M. Free admission on Sunday. Call (816) 233–7003.

Family diners won't want to miss the home cooking and baking available at **Jerre Anne Cafeteria and Bakery,** 2640 Mitchell Avenue. For more than sixty-five years, this restaurant has provided an ever-changing

See the house where Jesse James lived and died, behind the engaging Patee House Museum in St. Joseph. (Photo by Jane Cosby)

selection of entrees, vegetable dishes, salads, and desserts. Open Tuesday through Saturday 11:00 A.M. to 7:00 P.M. Call (816) 232–6585.

The third weekend in August marks the celebration of **Trails West!,** held at Civic Center Park, 11th and Frederick Avenues. This festival features an arts-and-crafts show, musical entertainment, lectures, melodramas, rousing historical reenactments, food booths, and children's activities including an art tent with hands-on art projects and performances by jugglers and magicians. It's a great weekend of inexpensive entertainment for the whole family. Call (816) 233–0231. The **Apple Blossom Festival,** held the first weekend in May, is a city-wide event with an Apple Blossom Parade, concerts, dances, and a softball tournament. For information about times and locations call (816) 233–8549 or (816) 271–1442.

The city has beautiful scenic drives that wind for 26 miles and connect several city parks. Visit 163-acre **Krug Park** at St. Joseph Avenue and Krug Park Place, where you'll find scenic hiking trails, picnic areas, a castle, and a playground. The park also has a North American animal exhibit with buffalo, deer, and longhorn cattle. During the month of December the park is lighted to create a dazzling drive-through display. The holiday drive-through is open daily from dark until 10:00 P.M. Donations are requested. Call (816) 271–5500.

From Southwest Parkway visit the **King Hill Overlook** on King Hill Drive and get a breathtaking view of the south side of the city and eastern Kansas. This area was once a Native American ceremonial ground. **Huston Wyeth Park,** at Poulin and Elwood Streets, is located on the river bluffs and provides a great view of the point where wagon trains crossed the Missouri River to begin the journey west. The picnic areas in the park are good vantage points for watching the river.

Western shoppers can find plenty of places to browse in town. Visit the **Silver Fox Indian Trading Post,** 5104 King Hill Avenue, to see hundreds of Native American items and artifacts including pottery, bolos, collar tips, pipes, and hat bands. Call (816) 238–7560. **St. Joe Boot,** located at the Belt Highway and Highway 36, has Western fashions and accessories, in addition to more than 4,000 boots for men, women, and children. Call (816) 232–8128. Or step back in time and see custom saddles being made the way they were at the turn of the century, at **Bill's Saddlery,** 1205 South 9th Street, which also sells hand-crafted leather goods, bags, belts, and purses. Call (816) 279–7392. The **Stetson Hat Factory Outlet,** 3601 South Leonard Road, offers Western felt and straw hats, dress hats, and caps of all types. Call (816) 233–3286.

Would-be cowhands can get practice and instruction at the **Draggin B Ranch,** located 6 miles north of the city, 12261 County Road 360. Horsemanship instruction is available for all skill levels, including beginners. You can ride on scenic country trails, with horse-drawn hayrides and chuck-wagon cookouts. Reservations required. For rates and availability call (816) 324–4906.

MOUND CITY

As you travel north along the Missouri River, you'll notice the rural character of the countryside that makes the northwestern corner of the state excellent for wildlife viewing and outdoor recreation. **Squaw Creek National Wildlife Refuge,** located a few miles south of town on Highway

159, is an opportunity that shouldn't be missed. It is one of the best locations in the state for year-round wildlife viewing. Snow geese, Canada geese, mallards, white pelicans, eagles, and other types of birds stop off here during their fall and spring migrations, providing you with a chance to observe the noisy confusion and the awesome sight. At these times there are hundreds of thousands of waterfowl feeding and resting on the marshes. This area attracts more wintering bald eagles than any other area in the state, possibly in the lower forty-eight states.

Start at the refuge headquarters to get information, and be sure to bring binoculars so you can spot birds and wildlife from afar. There is an auto road that circles the marsh and pools, providing excellent viewing from the comfort of your car. Hiking trails, wayside exhibits, and a viewing tower are also on-site. Fall and spring are the best times to observe migrating populations of waterfowl, which you will see flying in lines strung out across the sky for miles around the refuge. Sunrise and sunset are the most active times of day for the wildlife. No admission charge. Center is open Monday through Friday 7:30 A.M. to 4:00 P.M. Refuge is open daily from sunrise to sunset. Call (816) 442–3187.

The refuge celebrates **Eagle Days** during December or January of every year. During this time you can view hundreds of bald eagles and learn about the comeback of our national symbol. The event includes guided eagle tours, a movie about eagles, captive eagles on display, and various exhibits. Call (816) 442–3187.

Camping and picnicking are not allowed in the refuge, but you can find facilities at nearby **Big Lake State Park,** located 11 miles southwest of town on Highway 111. This 625-acre park includes a natural oxbow lake formed when the Missouri River shifted course. The lake is popular for boating and waterskiing, and there are eighty campsites, housekeeping cottages, a swimming pool, and a twenty-two-unit motel and dining lodge in the park. Call (816) 442–3770.

SAVANNAH

You can escape to the country at **Ol' MacDonalds Farm,** 15603 County Road 344. Camping facilities are available for trailers, tents, and recreational vehicles. You can fish, hike, or take a trail ride on horseback. The

JANE'S TOP ANNUAL EVENTS IN THE NORTHWEST REGION

Snake Saturday Parade and Celebration, March, North Kansas City, (816) 274–6000 or (816) 471–7463

Children's Day, June, Missouri Town 1855, Blue Springs, (816) 795–8200, ext. 1260

Trails West!, August, St. Joseph, (816) 233–0231

Santa-Cali-Gon Days, Labor Day Weekend, Independence, (816) 252–4745

Jesse James Festival, September, Kearney, (816) 968–9680

Southside Fall Festival Rodeo Round-up, September, St. Joseph, (816) 238–1450

American Royal Livestock, Horse Show and Rodeo, October through November, Kansas City (816) 221–7979 or (816) 221–9800

Plaza Lighting Ceremony and Lighting Display, Thanksgiving evening through December, Kansas City, (816) 753–0100

Winter Festival, Thanksgiving weekend, Jamesport, (816) 684–6146

ninety-acre facility includes a swimming pool, dining room, general store, and concession stand. For reservations and rates call (816) 324–6447.

CAMERON

Heading east you'll find **Wallace State Park,** located 6 miles south of town off Highway 35, which offers rugged wooded terrain that contrasts with the rolling farmland of this part of the state. The park has four of the prettiest and most varied hiking trails in the region, offering dense woods, open meadows, and streams. There are sixty-eight campsites, and small

Lake Allaman offers swimming, fishing, and boating for electric motorboats only. Call (816) 632–3745.

JAMESPORT

As you drive north and approach this town, which is the largest Amish community in the state, you'll pass carriages and farmers tilling the land with horse-drawn equipment. The Old Order Amish who live in this area maintain a nineteenth-century lifestyle and shun modern conveniences and technology. You and your kids can enjoy the charm of stepping back in time among people who aren't just pretending. The town has two-dozen specialty craft stores, including a carriage store and rug and broom store, where you can watch craftspeople at work. There are several excellent restaurants and bakeries where you can buy home-baked meals and goodies. Many of the farms in the area sell quilts, homemade candy and bread, crafts, furniture, and clothing. Get a map in one of the stores in town and go exploring. Amish stores are closed on Thursday and Sunday. Call (816) 684–6146 or (816) 684–6111.

TRENTON

North Central Missouri College and the Grundy County Friends of the Arts cooperate to bring live family productions to this small town. The **Arts and You** series offers music concerts, children's theater, and individual performing artists from August through April at various community locations. For a schedule of events and ticket prices call (816) 359–4324.

LACLEDE

You can visit the **Gen. John J. Pershing Boyhood Home,** located 1 mile north of town on Highway 5, and see where the highest-ranking military officer in United States history grew up. The one-room school where he taught school is also on the site. Small fee for tours. For hours call (816) 963–2525. **Pershing State Park,** on Highway 130, has thirty-eight campsites, two small lakes, and hiking trails along Locust Creek. An interpretive boardwalk through a wetland area offers an interesting look at this natural habitat. Call (816) 963–2299.

The **Locust Creek Covered Bridge State Historic Site,** located 3 miles west of town off Highway 36, protects the longest remaining covered bridge in the state. When the creek channel changed after World War II, the bridge was left high and dry. A footbridge makes it accessible to hikers. Call (816) 963–2525.

There are two extensive wetland areas close to town that provide outdoor recreation and prime opportunities to watch waterfowl, shorebirds, bald eagles, and aquatic mammals such as river otters and muskrat. **Fountain Grove Conservation Area,** with an area of more than 7,000 acres, offers primitive camping, hiking, small boating, and an auto tour route. To reach the area take County Road W south from Highway 36 and drive 5 miles to the entrance. Call (816) 646–6122.

Swan Lake National Wildlife Refuge covers more than 10,000 acres and has a visitor center where you can get information and an observation tower where you can get a great view. To reach the area take Highway 139 south 12 miles, then take County Road RA south to the refuge entrance. Call (816) 856–3323. At both areas follow the levees, service roads, and trails for the best viewing. These areas are restricted to the public during waterfowl hunting season, from October 15 until mid-February, so call ahead during that time for specific availability.

If your family is on a quest for wide-open spaces, head north on Highway 5. You'll see some of the least-populated areas and least-traveled roads in the state. Fewer than 150 cars a day use the northern end of this highway as it heads into Iowa.

MACON

In this eastern part of the region, **Long Branch Lake,** just west of town, offers outdoor recreation such as boating, skiing, camping, fishing and hunting. A visitor center on Highway 36 has displays on the construction of the lake and on the wildlife in the area. **Long Branch State Park** has forty campsites, a sand beach for swimming, boat-launching facilities, and a full-service marina. Call (816) 773–5229.

KIRKSVILLE

To the north is the college town of Kirksville, which plays host to several events that attract visitors from all over the region. June brings the largest rodeo in this part of the state, the **El Kadir Shrine Club Rodeo.** July is the **NEMO District Fair,** featuring big-name entertainment, a demolition derby, 4-H and FFA exhibits, hot-air balloons, and carnival rides. And in September, high-school students come from all over the area to compete in the **High School Rodeo.** For dates and information on these events call (816) 665–3766.

Family entertainment is available at the **Chariton Valley Opry,** Highway 6, which offers country music and comedy. For show times and ticket prices call (816) 665–3085.

Just west of town is **Thousand Hills State Park,** Highway 6 to Highway 157. This 3,200-acre wooded park surrounds Forest Lake and offers camping, swimming, hiking, boating, and picnic facilities. It has a full-service marina, cabins, and a dining lodge. The park has a petroglyph site believed to be part of ceremonial grounds used by Native people from 1000 to 1600 A.D., complete with original rock carvings. Summer activities include evening programs, nature hikes, pontoon boat rides, a petroglyph open house held every Saturday, and interpretive boat tours of the lake on Sunday afternoons. Call (816) 665–6995.

GENERAL INDEX

A

Albrecht-Kemper Museum of Art, 137
Alley Spring, 53
Alley Spring Grist Mill, 53
American Heartland Theater, 122
American Royal Livestock, Horse
    Show and Rodeo, 117
American Royal Museum and
    Visitor Center, 117
American Saddle Horse Museum, 3
America's National Parks, 18
Amigetti's Bakery, 22
Amtrak, 25, 102, 105
Anheuser-Busch Brewery
    Tour Center, 17
Apple Blossom Festival, 138
Apple Butter Festival, 36
Applefest Celebration, 134
Arabia Steamboat Museum, 118
Arrow Point Archery, 12
Arrow Rock State Historic Site, 110
Arts and You, 142
Audrain Country School, 1
Audrain Historical Society at
    Graceland, 2
August A. Busch Memorial
    Conservation Area, 8

B

Baldknobbers Jamboree, 69
Bass Pro Shops Outdoor World, 61
Battle of Lexington State
    Historic Site, 129
Becky Thatcher Book and
    Gift Shop, 5
Bee Tree Park, 34
Benjamin Ranch, 123
Bennett Spring State Park, 55

Benton County Museum, 43
Big Bay, 81
Big Boy's Restaurant, 106
Big Cedar Lodge, 79
Big Foot 4X4 Inc., 12
Big Lake State Park, 140
Big Oak Tree State Park, 42
Big Shot Family Action Park, 97
Big Sugar Creek, 81
Big Surf Water Park, 96
Bill's Saddlery, 139
Blue Springs Lake, 124
Bluff Dwellers' Cave, 82
Bluffwoods Conservation Area, 134
Bob Kramer Marionette
    Theater, 18
Bolduc House, 39
Bollinger Mill State Historic Site, 40
Bonne Terre Mine, 47
Boone County Fair and
    Horse Show, 109
Boonesfield Village, 9
Boone's Lick State Historic
    Site, 110
Bootheel Youth Museum, 43
Bothwell Lodge State Historic
    Site, 111
Branson Cafe, 76
Branson Scenic Railway, 75
Branson Trout Dock, 75
Branson's Royalty, 69
Braschler Music Show, 69
Bridal Cave, 96
Bucks and Spurs Ranch, 66
Bull Shoals Lake, 66
Burr Oak Woods Conservation
    Nature Center, 126
Busch Stadium, 16

V

VanBurch and Wellford, 68

Village Days, 65

W

Wabash Frisco and Pacific Mini Steam
    Railway, 27

Wallace State Park, 141

Walnut Festival, 92

Walters Boone County Historical
    Museum and Visitors Center, 108

Washington State Park, 36

Washington Town and
    Country Fair, 105

Watkins Mill State Park, 132

Wayside Park Trail, 54

Weldon Spring Conservation Area, 8

West Plains Civic Center, 59

West Plains Motor Speedway, 54

Weston Bend State Park, 134

Westport, 122

Whiteman Air Force Base, 112

White Water, 72

Wilson's Creek National
    Battlefield, 63

Winston Churchill Memorial and
    Library, 106

Wolf Sanctuary, 32

Woofie's, 26

Worlds of Fun, 130

Y

Yogi Bear's Jellystone Park
    Camp-Resort, 31

ACTIVITIES INDEX

MUSEUMS AND ART
GALLERIES

HISTORIC SITES
AND HOMES

THEATERS, MUSIC SHOWS, AND CULTURAL EVENTS

RESTAURANTS AND SHOPPING

AMUSEMENT PARKS AND FAMILY ACTIVITY CENTERS

SPORTS AND ARENAS

ANIMALS, ZOOS AND NATURE CENTERS

ACCOMMODATIONS

TRANSPORTATION
AND RIDES

LAKES AND RIVERS